AF392063

The Top 20 Jobs in Digital

Julien Oudart has more than 20 years of experience in digital marketing, working in both large companies and start-ups. After having spent ten years in the marketing departments of Orange and Vodafone in Brussels, London and Tokyo, Julien was involved in developing start-ups in ad tech. In 2011, he created NukeSuite, a social marketing software editor which was subsequently sold to the Webeda group in 2016. Today Julien lives in Los Angeles.

Clément Vérité works for the New York Times in Paris as a revenue analyst on digital monetization strategy. Previously, Clément was a content manager in a company specializing in the recruitment of C-suites and business executives. He has also worked as a journalist for various press media.

The Top 20 Jobs in Digital

A reference guide to the top jobs in the digital ecosystem based on the accounts of 60 experts in more than 15 countries

Julien Oudart

Clément Vérité

Copyright © Julien Oudart and Clément Vérité, July 2020
Los Angeles, California and Paris, France
1st edition

Cover: Céline Bouchez

ISBN: 978-2-9572290-1-7

Table of Contents

Foreword

Why Write This Book?

In the last few years, the labor market has seen the arrival of a number of new jobs related to the digitalization of businesses such as data analyst, user experience (UX) designer and growth marketer to name but a few.

Who can clearly explain what is involved from day-to-day in these new jobs? What information is available to explain the required qualities and skills? How can one be better informed as to how these new jobs are going to evolve?

Little, if any, information exists about what these jobs actually entail on a daily basis, what the required skill sets are and what the prospects are of further development in the medium and long terms. It is in this context and with these questions in mind that we worked on this book for anyone who has an interest in digital technology and who needs to understand what is involved for each of these jobs. The main aim of this book is therefore to provide as many pointers as possible in order to help the reader better understand the main business actors, both now and in the future.

It therefore seemed natural to hear directly from the professionals, based on a series of interviews which allowed us to examine in detail each job and to better understand how these jobs will develop and evolve in the future.

Who is This Book Aimed at?

This book is aimed at those who want to better find their way around the digital world or those wishing to become a part of it.

The digitalization of jobs is leading to increased linkages between sales and marketing positions and technical functions. Mathematicians or statisticians can now be recruited for data processing jobs in commercial teams in start-ups; a business school graduate who knows how to code can apply for a job in a team of data analysts. It is for this reason that the jobs we have listed will be of interest to graduates in business, engineering, design and communications but also to those coming from psychology or literature.

We also hope that this work will bring value to anyone already working in the digital sector who wishes to gain a better understanding of their industry, either out of simple curiosity to know more about the sector or as a means to change jobs: the digital industry is constantly evolving and creating new opportunities.

Our wish is that this book is accessible to as many people as possible and can be read by anyone who has no particular knowledge of this field but who wishes to discover the world of digital technology through its various jobs.

How Was This Book Developed?

Starting from the simple webmaster at the beginning of the 2000s, the last 15 years have seen the growth of a multitude of new jobs as the practices and services linked to digitalization have matured. The constant fragmentation of jobs and the evolution of new roles can sometimes make it difficult to keep up with them.

We wanted to approach this issue by using the empirical vision (and experience) of professionals in the digital sector and this work is largely based on the dozens of interviews we carried out. We selected the interviewees based on the relevance of their job functions and of the companies they work for, as well as for the originality of their accounts. Our ultimate goal is to provide readers with varied, concrete and practical information as to what each job actually entails on a day-to-day basis.

The world of digital technology is a globalized one and for this reason we conducted the interviews across a wide range of countries (17 in total): 18% of the interviewees work in the United States, 17% in France, 15% in Asia and 15% in the United Kingdom. A detailed list is provided as an appendix.

Choosing the Jobs

Choosing the top 20 jobs we wanted to cover was the subject of much debate, in which our contacts involved in the sector participated and with whom we exchanged ideas in the preparation of this book.

We focused on the most relevant jobs which, based on our own experience, represent a significant volume of employment in the sector, both now and in the (very) near future.

The list is, of course, non-exhaustive and some may be disappointed that their roles were not included. We have merged some jobs that share the same terminology or tasks in order to cover as many functions as possible.

The Digital Market

After first making an appearance at the end of the 1990s and growing in the 2000s, in recent years the underlying practices and actors in digital technology can now be considered to have reached a certain level of maturity.

The activity is clearly structured around a number of key actors such as audience holders (media groups, publishers and platforms), investors (VCs), start-ups, communications agencies, recruiters, public organizations, industrial groups and retail operators such as mass-market brands.

The current predominance of the digital industry can be attributed to the influence of 5 phenomena:

- **The advent of digital technology**: between 1960 and 2000, digital technology was already impacting our everyday lives via the use of household applications (domestic appliances and Hi-Fi) and transport (trains, planes and cars). Some people were already hooked on devices such as the Japanese cameras that swept the world in the 1980s. Despite this, digital technology, in particular when linked to electronics, was still practically unknown to most people until the 2000s. Things began to move faster from the middle of the 2000s, mainly due to the commercialization of the iPhone which put a device full of electronics into the pockets of more and more people. The simultaneous surge of content (www), containers (broadband networks) and devices (such as the iPhone) triggered an explosion in usage. It also led to digital technology becoming a subject about which we read daily and whose products we all purchase. For most of us, digital technology has been transformed from a remote concept to a significant element in all our lives.

- **The democratization of usage**: the general public has seized enthusiastically upon the spread of digital technology, in particular on new products that are easy to use and which give real added value. Technological applications require enormous levels of investment to get started, which has led to companies (mainly American and Asian at this point) becoming global actors in just a few years. These giants have the means to commercially deploy applications rapidly. As a consequence, new products can be accessed by millions of users within a mere two years after their market launch (as an example, there are already 2.5 billion voice assistants in use in the world today - including those installed in our phones). It is also interesting to note that the growing appetite for the next wave of innovations has been driven by the dissemination of technological applications. More and more people are following with interest the next wave of digital technology that will make their lives easier, such as autonomous cars or innovations in transportation, health, environment and education.

- **The proliferation of data**: the mass use of technological devices has led to an exponential generation of data. The consulting firm CGI forecasts that 175 zettabytes (billions of billions) of data will be produced in 2025 compared to 33 zettabytes in 2018 - representing a five-fold increase in volume. All the main brands want to identify, collect, store and analyze these new big data sources in order to extract commercial value from them. One explanation for this explosion of data is that the economic pressure during the financial crisis of 2008-2014 caused businesses to forge closer ties with their customers by developing jobs in data acquisition as well as in customer relations and services. The appetite for using the information they collected has given rise to a new group of data-related jobs in the last few years which are constantly evolving as new privacy laws and regulations are introduced. The main aim of these new regulations, such as the G.D.P.R. (General Data Protection Regulation) in the European Economic Area, the e-Privacy act in Switzerland or the Consumer Privacy Act in California, is the protection of user privacy. These regulations have added to the ever-increasing attention on the use of data. They have also contributed to the creation or reinvention of jobs such as CPO (Chief Privacy Officer), CRM (Customer Relationship Manager) or data analyst.

- **Concentration of investment**: the innovation funding landscape has changed radically in the last 5 years. The number of actors (in particular those in investment funds) and the amounts of money injected have exploded to all-time highs. Public policies of the countries most committed to digital technology (for example Bpifrance and its label French Tech in France) followed suit by providing more and more support for start-ups. The corporate world has also been moving more quickly on this issue, more often than not motivated through a fear of missing the boat. There are now countless business incubators and accelerators launched by actors from sectors such as insurance, banking, transportation, retail and cosmetics. Combined with other factors, such as the growing desire among younger people to engage in digital technology, it has had an impact on the number of start-ups and jobs that have been created in recent years. The same trend can be observed in all the more developed countries – it is a global movement which started in the United States and then spread to Asia, Europe and now Africa. It can also be seen that in these regions, Series C and D type fundraising (of $50 million or more) have facilitated the emergence of start-ups, some of which have become unicorns and recruited tens of thousands of staff over periods of only 2 to 4 years.

- **Adapting the educational system**: no innovative and high-performance digital ecosystem can be built without a high-quality educational system. All of the great Digital Valleys have grown around one or more renowned universities - the Silicon Valley in the United States with Stanford, Bangalore University (BU) in India or in China with Shenzhen University (SZU). Digital marketing programs have been created in all universities and schools around the globe, and increasing numbers of speakers from the corporate world now share their knowledge with students who are ever more attracted to the world of start-ups. In addition, business school students now have the opportunity to learn the basics of coding via public or private training courses and engineering students can now move into jobs that focus more towards clients, such as data analysts, product owners or into marketing when they have completed a double degree program. Some initiatives, such as École 42 in Paris, and now also in a dozen other countries, use collaborative teaching methods similar to what is applied in the industry.

All of the actors in this ecosystem, whether they are digital natives or come from previous generations, are now very much aware of the impact of digitalization. As a result, they have invested in the creation of new business models based around digital products and services or have initiated their own digital transformations. This has obviously had a significant impact on the requirements for expertise and the creation of new jobs: the number of jobs increased by 43% in SEO (Search Engine Optimization) marketing and by 33% in content marketing between 2018 and 2019.

The Jobs

To get the most relevant and comprehensive vision of the 20 key jobs in the digital technology market, we assembled a simple matrix with 5 groups of main actors:

- **Brands**: whether public brands or retailers, their main objective is to reach their relevant audience in order to increase brand awareness and to convert prospects into clients.

- **Technology vendors**: developers of software and other technical solutions.

- **Service providers**: communication agencies and consulting firms, in particular related to IT.

- **Audience holders**: media groups and platforms such as the GAFA (Google, Amazon, Facebook, Apple).

- **Recruiters and investors**: these professions have changed radically since the arrival of digital technology.

The Job Matrix

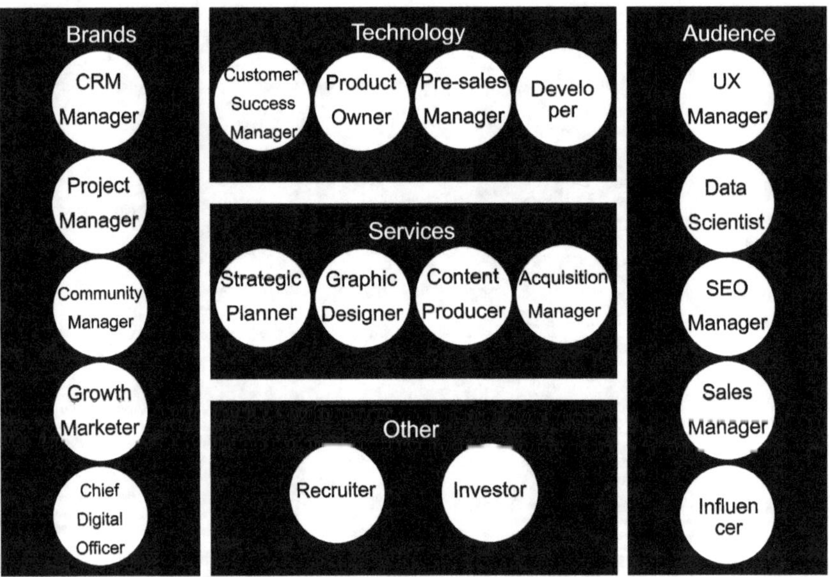

Below is a short description of each role:

- **The Customer Relationship Manager (CRM)** is responsible for the quality and the use of customer data.
- **The Project Manager** is responsible for the implementation and tracking of projects.
- **The Community Manager** is responsible for social network strategy and community development.
- **The Growth Marketer** is responsible for content marketing and generating new leads.
- **The Chief Digital Officer (CDO)** is responsible for the integration of digital and technology across all functions within a company.
- **The Customer Success Manager** is a cross between project manager and account manager, in charge of the management of the project and customer relations.
- **The Product Owner** is responsible for product strategy and development.
- **The Pre-sales Manager**'s role is between product manager, strategist and sales representative, and is the product guarantee with the sales teams.
- **The Developer** is responsible for the programming of front-ends, back-ends and IT architecture.
- **The Strategic Planner** defines communication strategy and planning within agencies, sales offices, trading desks or media teams.
- **The Graphic Designer** creates visuals.
- **The Content Producer** is responsible for the production of content such as texts, photographs, videos and audio.
- **The Acquisition Manager** is responsible for marketing campaigns, in particular to acquire new customers.
- **The UX Manager** is responsible for the development of interfaces and user experience.
- **The Data Scientist** manages data architecture and provides data analysis for brands, developers, agencies.
- **The Search Engine Optimization (SEO) Manager** is responsible for optimizing search engine positions and generating web traffic.
- **The Sales Manager** is in charge of the sales and marketing functions within an agency or for technical solution developers.
- **The Recruiter** specializes in recruiting staff in new technology, IT positions and start-ups.
- **The Investor** is an analyst in an investment fund or M&A bank.
- **The Influencer** has developed a personal audience, mainly on social networks and monetizes with brands.

The following biases chosen in constructing this matrix and job list should be highlighted:

- We focused on the analysis of operational functions and deliberately chose to exclude most executive functions.

- The job list does not include that of the entrepreneur whose role is definitely transverse and something of a jack-of-all-trades that overlaps with several other jobs.

- Each function may be carried out differently depending on the company in which it is performed. For this reason, a sales manager working in a software start-up would have radically different approaches, processes and interlocutors than a sales manager in a media group. In order to illustrate this diversity, we attempted to interview profiles that were representative of this diversity.

- The jobs listed are not 100% digital but due to the rapid and accelerating digitalization of companies across the spectrum, these functions are geared more and more to digital technology and tools.

- The ways of working and doing business are constantly evolving, an example of which is demonstrated by the rise of remote work. It is important to underline that all these functions may be carried out within a company structure as well as freelancing or remotely. For this reason, a number of the interviews were conducted with freelancers.

- Salaries were not discussed in the interviews as these vary greatly from country to country and according to the cost of living.

- The objective of this book is also to clarify the title of each of the functions within an ecosystem which has not quite reached its maturity and where it is common to find several titles for the same job. We have deliberately opted to use the broadest or most used terms of the industry (for example using product owner for product manager).

#1 CRM Manager

"You see marketers leading CRM teams but we will see more technical people leading this area in the future."

David Martin, Cabify

The customer relationship manager seeks to develop sales to its customers, whose contact points are increasingly digitalizing.

The CRM is responsible for data collection, data analysis and the operation of the customer database which is centralized in a customer relationship management (CRM) tool. This enables the launch of promotional campaigns, via email or SMS, the setting up of loyalty or retargeting programs, growing and improving the interaction between the brand and the customer. In recent years the job of CRM manager has evolved due to:

- The growing use of third-party external data, in order to have a broader vision of the market and more granular targeting. However, with new laws concerning privacy (of the G.D.P.R. type) being implemented, internal data is becoming, once again, pivotal in CRM brand strategies.

- There is a strong tendency to merge data that have a unique identifier (e.g. through collecting emails and phone numbers) with non-identified data (derived from cookies, for example) within the CDP (Customer Data Platform).

This means that CRM and media teams need to work more closely within organizations toward advertising investments.

Data concerning existing customers facilitates building target profiles and anticipating purchasing behaviors, sometimes with the help of predictive statistical models. This allows one to establish lookalike audiences and attract a larger customer base via organic (e.g. newsletters) or fee-paying levers (e.g. Facebook ads). This is an example of data onboarding.

It is also worth noting that despite the use of the word customer, the CRM generally includes the management of prospects (not only existing customers), and for this reason the term PRM, or prospect relationship manager, can also be used.

Jose Manuel Martin Sanchez
Title: CRM manager
Company: Fnac
City: Madrid
Age: 43

What is a successful CRM manager?

Jose Manuel: CRM means analyzing the company's sales and understanding consumer behaviors so that we can adapt our communication strategies accordingly. I think CRM should focus on customer behaviors; not what customers express - the latest studies in neuroscience suggest that 70% of the buying decision process comes from an unconscious perspective.

How do you measure success?

Jose Manuel: The higher the customer satisfaction, the better. One of the most relevant KPIs (Key Performance Indicator) we use is the NPS (Net Promoter Score), assessing the level of satisfaction and giving the number of brand ambassadors among the customer base. We also use frequency or spend per customer, churn rate, etc.

What profiles do you like for CRM managers?

Jose Manuel: CRM teams are really diverse but I think they need to have 3 key components: technical (IT), analytical and operational (such as brand managers, layout designers, etc.). Due to the importance of data analysis in making decisions, I like candidates with a solid statistical or mathematical background and good technical skills in order to anticipate the challenges in implementing a project, since technology is continuing to grow exponentially. It is essential to know how to use database management systems, business intelligence tools such as MicroStrategy, Oracle BI, Google analytics and also different communication channels and email marketing tools such as Salesforce, Eloqua, Neolane, etc.

David Martin
Title: Head of CRM
Company: Cabify
City: Madrid
Age: 44

What is your job?

David: Cabify is a ridesharing app in Spain and my objective is to increase the engagement of our users through communication campaigns. I am responsible for all the company's communication channels: email, push notifications from the app, in-app messages and SMS. We work on all stages of the customer lifecycle as well as the various audiences, from the drivers to the riders.

What software do you use most for your activity?

David: At Cabify, I use Braze a lot - a CRM software tool that helps improve engagement and conversations with customers. We also use Tableau, a data analytics and visualization tool, as well as Trello for managing and organizing our projects.

What challenges will CRM face in the future?

David: I think communicating with customers will always be important. Artificial intelligence is becoming an essential component in almost every business process, so it's important to take advantage of these new technologies. We need to help the machine learn as much as possible. On the other hand, if you don't have a technical or analytical vision, then you will need to develop one. The challenge will be to mix the technical part with both the strategic and creative sides of a marketing job. Nowadays, you see marketers leading CRM teams but we will see more technical people leading this area in the future.

#2 Project Manager

"If you have led a project from beginning to end, managing different skills and personalities, then you can call yourself a project manager."

Carolina Nishino, MediaMonks

The role of a project manager is like that of the conductor of an orchestra - a coordinator. The objective is to carry out an operation over a few days or several months. The project manager guarantees the relevance and the proper execution of the project.

This position is found in almost every organization, whether it be a brand, an agency or firm of contractors. It is important to know precisely the missions to be completed because the job can change totally from one position to another.

The Agile method, where a project is split into several independent and achievable pieces, has become the mantra of project managers who represent the scrum masters. A project manager more often than not has no hierarchical power towards his interlocutors and needs to use his/her soft skills in order to influence the stakeholders and to ensure they comply with the brief. S/he also needs to be rigorous to ensure the project is delivered as was initially defined and within the set time frame. A project manager also requires a good working knowledge of market tools such as MS Project, Slack, Jira and Trello.

The lack of time and financial resources, the inconsistencies between the concept of the project and its implementation are recurrent obstacles that a project manager needs to overcome.

Project management is accessible to a wide range of profiles so there is often stiff competition for a job opening. The role is less specialized; therefore possibilities of evolution are more open.

Laura Delange
Title: Digital project manager
Company: AccorHotels
City: Paris
Age: 31

Can you describe your job in a few words?

Laura: I am a project manager in the Client Value team in the AccorHotels Loyalty Program Business Unit. Our main objective is to increase client loyalty so customers will re-book nights in our hotels. I develop new offers according to our market segments within a predefined communication plan. The objective is to develop the value of every single client. I create new campaigns within the budget and timeframe given to me. My daily tasks include driving communication and translation agencies (30%), coordination with our international teams (20%), content redaction (email, display ads 20%), providing communication material (20%) and testing user experience (10%).

What tools do you use?

Laura: The Microsoft Office pack (Word, Excel, Powerpoint), some content management platforms such as Adobe Experience Manager, Wise and also Adobe Photoshop.

How do you think your job is going to evolve?

Laura: My position is changing rapidly through the introduction of agile project management methods and more reactivity and flexibility are required. The objective is that a project can be broken down in small sub-projects with ever shorter deadlines.

Solana Dominguez
Title: Project manager
Company: Cognizant
City: Buenos Aires
Age: 47

Can you describe your job?

Solana: As a project manager my duty is to schedule daily meetings with the team and customer, make sure the client agrees on what has been completed to date, mitigate risks and monitor the technical teams. Meetings take up most of my time. You need to report on progress, announce changes, pull reports, track issue logs, create or edit documentation, constantly follow-up on tasks assigned to the team. I use Microsoft Excel, Calendars (to set up reminders and meetings) as well as sticky notes (it may sound unprofessional or old school, but I do use them a lot!).

What experience do you have and what profile should a good candidate have?

Solana: I graduated from university with a Bachelor of Fine Arts. I had plenty of work experience. At a young age I started working as a secretary then I got the opportunity to start working at IBM where I began to help project managers carry out their work and I was myself then promoted to project manager. To be a good candidate requires several skills such as leadership, excellent communication, efficiency, being proactive, detail-oriented and punctual.

How do you see your job in the future?

Solana: The world of a project manager is huge. The methodologies are continuously changing, so I see myself training and learning new skills.

Carolina Nishino
Title: Project manager
Company: MediaMonks
City: São Paulo
Age: 26

What is your background?

Carolina: I graduated as a product designer, where one has to manage project iterations in order to complete a task. This made me de facto a project manager. If you have led a project from beginning to end, managing different skills and personalities, then you can call yourself a project manager.

Who do you work with?

Carolina: I usually report to the client and my boss. On a day-to-day basis, I work with designers, illustrators, developers, copywriters, QA (Quality Assurance) specialists among others. My job also requires me to master tools such as Asana, BaseCamp for project management, Sketch or Figma for design.

What trends do you see in project management?

Carolina: From my point of view, having someone with a generalist skill set, who is continuously learning to see the big picture will always be important, even if, every now and then, people need to focus and specialize in a particular area. Machines can be trained to get from one point to the other, but I don't think they will get to replace the orchestrator that soon.

Carlo Mobrack
Title: Project manager
Company: IBM
City: Paris
Age: 47

How do you spend a day as project manager?

Carlo: I spend my day working on project management meetings, technical reports, resource planning, statistics, and communications.

What qualities are needed for a project manager?

Carlo: I would say soft skills such as patience, knowing how to deal with angry clients and to always be smiling. You need to keep your common sense, have some good knowledge in management and strong communication skills. Technical skills are useful but not always necessarily a must.

How do you see your job and your career evolution?

Carlo: I will soon be taking early retirement! But generally speaking, my position is meant to rely more on technical tools in the near future.

#3 Community Manager

"I see this job playing a bigger role in how companies are run in the future."

Georgia Ingram, Debenhams

The role of the community manager (CM) is to recruit and animate an online brand community and to manage public interactions with its audiences such as fans and followers.

The CM projects the identity and image of the brand. The role evolved along with the growth of social network audiences and it requires the following skill set:

- Good working knowledge of the relevant platforms such as Facebook, Instagram, LinkedIn...

- An excellent understanding of brand strategies as well as of the marketing, customer service and CRM teams s/he will be working with.

- Creative abilities in order to push a brand. Good general knowledge and digital culture are essential.

- Paying strong attention to detail as everything published becomes public. The quality of the work of a community manager must be reflected in the content. Being a CM does not mean spending the day on Facebook. It requires a rigorous approach in managing community feedback according to brand values.

As a result, the CM position tends to be an internal one rather than outsourced to an agency or a freelancer. A CM would generally have training in communications.

The role of CM is constantly evolving which reflects the continual evolution of the various social media platforms. A distinction should be drawn between a CM, who focuses on production and distribution, and a social media manager, who is generally in a more senior position and whose role is rather to oversee the strategy and its implementation.

Georgia Ingram
Title: Social media manager
Company: Debenhams
City: London
Age: 26

Can you describe your job?

Georgia: I manage the social and content budget, set the strategy and oversee the delivery of campaigns across all social channels. The goal is to increase the engagement and the reach of followers of the brand. On a day-to-day basis, I manage the publication calendar on social platforms, work on campaign concepts and strategy documents. I work with different agencies: media, content creation, influencers. I manage my team and report to the head of marketing.

What skills are required?

Georgia: Communication skills, creativity and some leadership ability.

What advice would you give when starting a career?

Georgia: Social media manager is a function that serves every area of the business from HR to product development. It's important to try to understand what they all do and how much effort you need to put in so that they get the social media coverage they require. You also need to remain diplomatic and ultimately tell the best story to the customer. Content is king. It is imperative to understand what works and doesn't work, which is why reporting is so important. Social media are becoming more and more important and I see this job playing a bigger role in how companies are run in the future.

Ariel Cruz Pizarro
Title: Community manager
Company: Freelance
City: Santiago de Chili
Age: 28

What's your job?

Ariel: I have 2 jobs for 2 different companies. I feed a blog, Recorrido that concerns public transport prices in Chile, and I am community manager for the company Buses Transantin. I work as a freelancer in both jobs.

What are your objectives?

Ariel: For the blog my goal is to create quality content for the brand in order to generate more traffic. We help solve client issues and concerns. We sell bus tickets, so I write articles about bus companies, touristic places, etc. For the community management aspect, I provide information on the schedules of our trips, the quality of service, show the interior of buses and answer any questions.

What do you think helps being successful in this job?

Ariel: You need empathy in order to understand the needs of travelers, even without having travelled to that place yourself. You need to be creative and answer questions in a friendly and relevant way. The ability to write well and to take pictures is important. You need to be patient. I think the most important thing in my position is that I know the industry well. This would be my advice: get to know the market during the first months in your job.

Javier Del Campo
Title: Social media strategist
Company: World Wide Web Digital
City: Madrid
Age: 36

What is your role at WWW Digital?

Javier: WWW Digital is a social media agency in which I develop online and social media marketing strategies. Once the relationship with the clients has been consolidated, I remain their main point of contact.

What is a typical day for you?

Javier: My 5 main activities are the supervision of the work of the community managers, pulling reports with results, organizing tasks for the whole team, budget control and updating clients on the status of their services. To achieve this, I use tools such as Asana, Slack or Hootsuite.

What advice would you give to a newbie?

Javier: The best advice I could give him/her comes from a movie called "The Martian", in which Matt Damon is able to survive alone on Mars and return to earth. Years later, a student asks him how he was able to solve all the problems and his answer is: "*You solve one problem, and you solve the next one, and then the next*". I tell my new employees the same thing: deal with one problem at a time.

#4 Growth Marketer

"Develop a growth mindset: be keen to try out new things, be patient enough to see them through and be willing to learn from them."

James Arnall, Perkbox

The growth marketer job first appeared in the United States at the beginning of the 2010s and was first called growth hacker to emphasize the fact that it relies above all on the ability to open up a field of possibilities by exploiting the limits of tools, such as emails and LinkedIn. As this role gained importance in organizations, the more politically correct term of growth marketer took over. Nevertheless, growth marketing, as defined below by Brice Maurin from Deux.io, *"is the Agile method applied to marketing"*. It means working flexibly and iteratively, using results to continually improve the service. It also involves being constantly aware of the latest technologies and tools in order to push back the boundaries of personalized marketing.

Growth marketer is a new role that was created by start-ups that offered Software-as-a-Service (SaaS) tools. Their aim was to develop efficient methods and quick wins - often on the borderline of legality – in order to increase the number of customers at a reduced cost without having to launch acquisition campaigns (paid media) and classic levers such as ads on Google or Facebook.

This job now extends to organizations such as agencies which recruit this type of profile to support their customers or the marketing departments wanting to make their digital marketing teams more flexible. Until recently, this job was mostly performed in a B2B (business-to-business) context.

The heart of the growth marketer profession usually goes hand in hand with inbound marketing strategies or attracting audiences through the creation and dissemination of content and marketing automation. For example, the creation of databases coupled with an acquisition strategy in a push, sequenced and multi-channel mode.

This new role, which is a cross between technology and marketing, often requires hybrid profiles such as engineers who have an interest in online marketing methods or, frequently, digital marketers who have some knowledge of coding, data architecture and database management.

This position requires a solid grasp of the most popular web tools such as LinkedIn and Facebook but also the myriad other new tools such as Segment.io, Lusha and Drift that appear every month. The role requires vigilance in spotting new trends and regularly testing out new solutions. Recent years have seen an increase in training for growth marketers which are aimed at marketing professionals.

Jean-Baptiste Trahin
Title: Senior product & growth manager
Company: Adobe
City: San Francisco
Age: 31

What is your background?

JB: I worked in sales in the finance industry before moving into business development for a start-up incubator. After creating my own company, I joined Twenty20, an American start-up bought by Envato. I have been a senior growth product manager at Adobe for 2 years now and I currently manage an experimentation roadmap on Adobe Photoshop with a focus on engagement and retention.

What does it mean concretely?

JB: I analyze the data on live experiments, check on team members, on work in progress, solve challenges we meet, research on what to experiment next and communicate about our experimentation roadmaps to partners.

What advice would you give to the next growth marketer?

JB: Start at the very bottom. Find a start-up that just raised money and go get your hands in all aspects of the business. Find a project you really care about and take it from start to finish. Be proud of the mistakes you make, talk about them, learn from them.

James Arnall
Title: Marketing director
Company: Perkbox
City: London
Age: 31

What is your job?

James: Perkbox is a European leader in employee perks for small and medium-sized enterprises (SMEs). We only recruit our clients through digital. I lead a team of 25 marketers, responsible for Perkbox's global acquisition strategy, driving growth and supporting revenue goals for the business. I report to the COO and work closely with the sales team for which we generate leads.

What is required to be a good growth marketer?

James: Show empathy, remain calm throughout difficult times but also develop a growth mindset: be keen to try out new things, be patient enough to see them through and be willing to learn from them.

How do you see this job change in the long run?

James: As we look to launch globally, I am excited to see what opportunities will come. With continued growth, my role may become solely focused on one given region. I may have my own company one day but I know there is still plenty more for me to learn at Perkbox and plenty more for me to sink my teeth into.

Brice Maurin
Title: C.E.O.
Company: Deux.io
City: Paris
Age: 38

How would you define a growth marketer?

Brice: Deux.io was one of the first growth marketing companies launched in Paris. We have witnessed the evolution of digital marketing in the last 5 years. On one hand, there is group or community management (broadcast) and, on the other, personalized marketing (unicast). The latter helps you communicate with clients in a targeted and customized manner. Growth marketing means the ability to leverage data and technology to accelerate this personalization within reasonable budgets.

What does s/he do all day?

Brice: Growth marketing is the Agile method applied to marketing. You therefore always have to be in benchmark and test modes. First you test, then the objective is to automate the tasks when you have found an efficient model. My team is made of 3 different profiles: those who define and validate the strategy and the plan with the clients; the operational people identify, test and launch solutions and developers who build scalable platforms.

How do you see growth marketing evolve?

Brice: Growth marketing is a method and a spirit before being a job. I believe this method is now spreading across all company functions – and only the most agile will survive. Today's growth marketer will not exist in its current form in 5 years. It will have reincarnated into a growth strategist or growth campaign manager within all marketing business units.

#5 Chief Digital Officer

"Be able to connect the dots between business, human needs and technology."

Omar Odino, Design Group Italia

The role of chief digital officer (CDO) covers different areas and types of responsibilities depending on the type of company s/he works for. A CDO could be responsible for business development for a purely digital player such as an online retailer for example. Often the role assumes more importance in companies that run along more traditional business lines and is responsible for the digital transformation in its broader sense at all levels including HR, finance and marketing.

More specifically the role entails integrating digitalization with the global strategy and internal processes in order for the organization to find a model that will enable it to better respond to new entrants or to changes in its business model.

Most medium or large organizations now have a CDO. This tends to be a senior profile that needs to have an overall perspective of the whole business as well as a thorough knowledge of new technologies in order to make improvements to the existing business model.

The role of the CDO will often be to lead in-house teams in reorganizations and the introduction of new processes which can result in strong internal resistance.

The CDO usually reports directly to top management and will require their full support without which the mission cannot succeed.

Omar Odino
Title: Chief digital officer
Company: Design Group Italia
City: Milan
Age: 42

Where did you work before becoming a CDO?

Omar. I first worked in a digital agency, Nurun (Razorfish), and then for Publicis, and MRM in Milan. I started as a CDO at Wunderman Thompson in 2010 to help the agency spread digital skills across the company.

What skills are sought after in a CDO?

Omar. I think that a good candidate for the role of CDO needs to be able to connect the dots between business, human needs and technology. A design thinking mindset is very important, considering the complexity that many companies have to manage across all areas of their organization.

How do you turn actions into success?

Omar. I bring the latest innovations to my company clients. I work with different resources and professionals ranging from digital consultants, UX and UI designers, product designers, IT specialists, software developers. I need to make sure these skills bring value to all departments across the organization including HR and Marketing.

Waël Benkerrour
Title: Chief digital officer
Company: Galeries Lafayette
City: Shanghai
Age: 31

How did you end up becoming a CDO?

Waël: I worked for 5 years at Galeries Lafayette, in Paris in the strategy and finance department. I wanted a more operational job, so I started to develop our digital business in China going back and forth between Europe and Asia before moving here.

Can you describe your role?

Waël: We are launching a company within the company itself. Our mission is to support the brick-and-mortar business through digital - mostly through the launch of our e-commerce platform. We had to analyze the market, develop our strategy and then launch across all local platforms as well as our own CRM project. To do that we had to recruit some local expertise and we will continue to do so.

Where do you stand in the overall organization?

Waël: : I report to the Galeries Lafayette International commercial director - he is a member of the board. I mostly work with people at the Paris HQ as well as with the China operations director (marketing, retail, merchandising). His team has a strong knowledge of the local business that we can rely on..

Sophie Viger: Technology, not without women!

Sophie Viger is the managing director of 42, a disruptive computer programming school.

Ada Lovelace, Grace Hooper, Margaret Hamilton, Kathleen Booth, Barbara Liskov, to name just a few... These are all exceptional women who have gone down in history and strongly underline that at the very beginnings of IT, women were a force to be reckoned with. Far from being mere bit-part players, they were at the foreground and their contributions spearheaded major breakthroughs. Our collective memory has forgotten the pioneering and innovative role they played.

Whereas they were numerous in the high-tech professions during the 1950s and 1960s, today only 15% women hold these positions. In the span of a few years, they have let themselves be progressively swept aside in a field they initially excelled in but then ended up believing it was not their rightful place. Worse than that, they started believing they did not like IT, which goes to show how deep-rooted popular belief is. This realization is even more alarming because at the time of the digital revolution, the IT executives are now board members. The absence of women contributes to their under-representation in senior positions.

Power is not given, it must be taken, so the saying goes. That is easy to say when inequalities are driven very early by the educational system and are reinforced by stereotypes so rooted that they have become part of our collective subconscious. Are girls more studious and literary? Are boys more math-prone and ambitious? These are popular misconceptions which have been long refuted but still persist despite the advances in neuroscience. Parents, family, school… It is vitally important to stem these prejudices because in sustaining them and by not stimulating scientific mindsets of girls, they start self-censoring at an age when the need for recognition and belonging are of such importance that it requires huge strength of character to swim against the current. According to a study published by Science of Learning, "*girls and boys showed significant gender similarities in neural functioning, indicating that boys and girls engage the same neural system during mathematics development*". In other words, if anyone doubted it, women are as capable of succeeding in science, technology, engineering and mathematics. The only differences are the environment in which boys and girls evolve, how they are stimulated and the clichés we project onto them, consciously or not.

At each step of their educational process, and starting as early as at the end of junior high school, children's paths are gendered and tacitly encourage the idea that boys and girls don't have the same ambitions. Unsurprisingly, when girls need to choose which courses to specialize in, they tend to be over-represented in the humanities/literature/philosophy, languages, economic and social sciences with 85% girls to 15% boys. On the other hand, in math/digital sciences/IT/physics/chemistry the ratio is 87% boys to 13% girls. School has imposed itself as the antechamber of segregation in the labor market: today only 17% of jobs are not gender-based, that is to say when men or women account for 40% to 60% of the work force.

Yet, the world is changing, which proves that gender conditioning is not a fate. The issue of the female condition is more and more at the heart of society, highlighting how unacceptable it is to differentiate according to gender. Working time, glass ceilings, pay inequalities, family management… Aren't we all born free and with equal rights?

Attitudes are shifting, in particular concerning the new generation of digital natives and I would like to think that the digital can contribute to reversing discriminatory processes and social exclusion in order to become the key for the transition toward a fairer and more inclusive society. Today, the digital is all around us, covering the whole economy and for this reason the digital industry needs women, as much as women need to be a force in these jobs of the future.

Besides the opportunities in a sector where talent is in shortage, it is unthinkable that the new technologies that change our lives are developed only by men and excluding 50% of the world population, under penalty of reproducing the sexist biases from which stem so many inequalities. Algorithms and A.I. are programmed by human beings who do no more than perpetuate our social codes inside technology. A report published by the Unesco, in May 2019, openly accuses apps such as Alexa, Cortana and Siri, of conveying sexist stereotypes. By giving their vocal assistants servile and obedient feminine voices in almost every language available, this insidiously perpetuates the image of the docile and dominated woman the world over and influences the perception men have of women, how they speak to them, etc. And, what is worse, how women perceive themselves. Role models are powerful levers and help protect from the Golem effect or the impostor syndrome. And examples of successful women, thankfully, are more and more visible and many organizations are committed to promote gender diversity in digital-related jobs. More generally, IT and its opportunities must be introduced in schools, without gender bias, in order to fight against educational stereotypes. Outdated models of male and female capabilities must be broken at every opportunity. It must be explained to girls and boys that IT is not gendered. What is more, the lack of awareness and limited perception that girls have of jobs in IT and engineering must be mitigated as they represent further obstacles in persuading girls to choose other paths.

At 42, we have defined a real plan of action of 35 concrete measures to sensitize junior high school and high school students, college students, women seeking work or going through a professional transition in order to help them broaden their horizons. We are striving to foster proper conditions for them to succeed while also ensuring that we develop a safe and comfortable working environment within which they feel respected and supported by the educational team as well as their peers. Their presence is not only legitimate, it is normal and natural for all of us. In 2018, we got rid, once and for all, of the 30-year age limit in order to participate in this program, and these initiatives are starting to bear fruit: there are now more women participating in and passing the selection tests. It was obvious, women turn towards opportunities in the digital industry at a later age, and our personalized teaching methods enable them to progress at their own rhythm while taking into consideration their personal constraints.

A new revolution must take place in order for women to be conscious of their own prejudices against IT, which is a means, not an end. Coding has become a key skill of the 21st Century, as is mastering one or more foreign languages. They need to open their eyes and go for it.

#6 Customer Success Manager

"Constantly challenge and question yourself, which requires a high degree of self-awareness - that is to say, constantly analyzing what you do well and what you are less comfortable with."

Nicolas Fatout, Adform

The function of customer success manager is relatively new in the digital sector and is probably one of the 5 most sought-after profiles on the market at the moment.

It is a hybrid function – somewhere between project manager and account manager – which has emerged with the proliferation of start-ups offering SaaS-based tool solutions.

The CSM takes over once the sales representative has signed up a customer to a new subscription for a product. S/he initially oversees the client's onboarding in the implementation of the project, which covers the creation of user accounts, defining the terms of use and guidelines, and can include training customer teams on how to use the tool. As the job title indicates, the role of the CSM is to ensure that the project is a success by optimizing the customer's use of the tool. A satisfied customer is more likely to renew a user license. The renewal rate (or conversely the churn rate) is therefore the main KPI for measuring the effectiveness of the CSM.

The customer success manager is not only a project manager but is also significantly involved in the renewal of customer contracts. S/he is usually paid a fixed basic salary plus a performance-based bonus which is directly related to his ability to keep a client at the end of the contractual period. As such, the role has many similarities to that of an account manager.

While often possessing a Business School profile (or its equivalent), the CSM must undoubtedly have an excellent grasp of the product but also master major technical subjects. The CSM is in constant contact with his product teams to monitor and follow-up on new customer requests or to escalate any issues encountered with the tool.

Takuji Kawamura
Title: Customer success manager
Company: Hubspot
City: Tokyo
Age: 33

What do you do at Hubspot?

Takuji: I am a CSM at Hubspot, the leading solution in CRM and Marketing Automation. My profile is atypical because I'm an engineer and my technical background really helps me in my current role. My job is to help customers use Hubspot and to retain them.

What do you do on a day-to-day basis?

Takuji: Half of my time is spent with clients with whom I am in constant contact by email or by phone. Much of my time is spent on internal coordination with the other teams.

What tools do you use daily?

Takuji: Health Score for the management of customer requests, in-house tools for managing tasks and a range of communication tools such as email and chat..

Stefania Fussi
Title: Customer success manager
Company: Yext
City: Milan
Age: 33

What is your profile and profession?

Stefania: I have an academic background in Economics and then spent 6 years in a social media agency and 3 years as a corporate social media manager. Yext provides a tool to optimize retailers' web presence; my role is to optimize the customers' use of our tools. I escalate any issues they encounter, develop direct relationships with customers and try to anticipate their needs. I also advise them so that they are able to communicate internally the ways Yext can help them. I collaborate with the sales, consulting and product development teams.

How is a typical day organized?

Stefania: I would say that I'm constantly monitoring trends to keep myself abreast of the market, provide customer support - that includes a quarterly review with everyone involved - and customer relation support.

Is the position set to change significantly in the coming years ?

Stefania: Yes, I think we are moving towards a more strategic consulting role with reduced customer support functions. Operational tasks will either be partly automated using specific tools or carried out by more junior profiles.

Nicolas Fatout
Title: Director of platform solutions
Company: Adform
City: Paris
Age: 29

What is your role at Adform?

Nicolas: Adform is an ad tech company with a technology that enables our customers to improve the way they target and reach their (future) customers on the web. I head up the team that manages Adform's customers and interact with all the different services of the company such as products, sales and marketing. I report to the Global Customer Service VP.

What is your typical day in the office?

Nicolas: I would say 50% of my time is spent mentoring members of my team and helping them find solutions to their problems. 20% is devoted to strategy: understanding future customer needs and finding the right tools. The remainder of my time is spent reporting and benchmarking.

What qualities does your job require?

Nicolas: The ability to listen (to the internal team and clients), empathy and trying to lead by example while adopting a human-centered approach. Above all, knowing how to constantly challenge and question yourself, which requires a high degree of self-awareness - that is to say, constantly analyzing what you do well and what you are less comfortable with.

#7 Product Owner

"If you don't like being in direct contact with a large number of interlocutors or prefer spending your time alone in front of your laptop, then this job isn't for you."

Cécile Eskenazi, Facebook

The position of product owner or product manager is not unique to digital marketing. In the digital industry this position is mostly found in start-ups or software companies.

The main role of the job is to define a product strategy which will lead to the roadmap – the product owners' bible – which describes the main new functionalities and indicates the direction the product will be heading over the next 12 to 18 months. This, of course, means that the product owner needs a good understanding of market trends and of the competitors. A particularly important task is to regularly update a competitive benchmark document.

On a more micro level, this position involves transforming the roadmap into functional specifications which the technical team will use to start developing. In some cases, the position may include that of a UX manager, in which case the product owner will also be responsible for defining the user interface of the product in collaboration with front-end developers who will build it. The product owner will then oversee the implementation by the technical team and the QA phase (tests) before production starts. S/he will then monitor the global performance of the platform and its features in order to improve the product, if need be.

This entails mastering a number of market tools such as Balsamique for the creation of wireframes and mock-ups or Jira to track the implementation of the functionalities with the technical team.

A product owner will typically have a business background or an engineering curriculum for a more technical training. The position is a central role which defines the identity and the characteristics of a product. Its importance is sometimes underestimated in start-ups and it is not always easy to find profiles that truly meet expectations.

Cécile Eskenazi
Title: Product manager
Company: Facebook
City: Menlo Park (U.S.A.)
Age: 41

What is your job within Facebook?

Cécile: I run a multidisciplinary team whose role is to launch new features on the Facebook app. I define objectives for the team, identify user requirements and coordinate the development of solutions to meet those requirements.

What is a typical day in the office?

Cécile: A product manager spends most of his/her time in meetings! If you don't like being in direct contact with a large number of interlocutors or prefer spending your time alone in front of your laptop, then this job isn't for you. I would say I spend around 50% of my time with the team or in one-on-ones, 30% responding to emails and 10% on strategy documents such as roadmaps or briefs.

My main interlocutor is my engineering manager. He drives my engineering team - about 15 people. I also work with product designers who help design features that will then be developed by engineers. I also often communicate with our data scientists and UX researchers whose jobs are to provide us with quantitative and qualitative insights on new client requirements and our product usage.

Are there any specificities linked to the way the company is run?

Cécile: At Facebook you do not directly have access to people's positions in the org chart so we can all propose new ideas and receive the same level of attention. For instance, my N+1 and I have the same title of product manager.

Malick Ndiaye
Title: Product marketing manager
Company: Knockout Gaming
City: Málaga
Age: 31

Can you describe your job for us?

Malick: At Knockout we build games and our objective is to create a unique and personalized digital experience for every single user. We work to increase our game usage and revenues generated by users. To do so we need to collect a great deal of data from users, digital or offline, and build automated patterns to respond in real time in a relevant manner..

What degree would you recommend to get a job like yours?

Malick: Education and degrees do not matter to me much. I look at the candidates' reasons for applying and their motivations. Softs skills are harder to acquire than knowing how to use Adobe Campaign or Salesforce.

What is the future of this job?

Malick: There will be ever more personalization as well as automation. The latter helps you save time and gives you more options to work on your strategy. Recently all the data have been stored and even though most of it never really gets used, it is available for analysis. Digital marketing will have to leverage this enormous quantity of data to reinvent itself and move away from all the dirty practices we have witnessed in the recent past.

It is also interesting to see that social media have also played a role in the way that the balance of power has changed between brands, clients and influencers, with influencers in the middle.

Marine Suttle
Title: Chief product officer
Company: The Boxoffice Company
City: Los Angeles
Age: 31

What is your role at The Box Office Company?

Marine: The Box Office Company (Webedia group) provides digital services to the film industry. I drive our product strategy. I work on the tools we develop to help our clients develop their own business. It is mostly about understanding needs, the market and always keeping up to date with where the competition is heading.

What skills does it require?

Marine: I would say not relying on what's already here and not being afraid of critical thinking. You also need to be well organized as the number of things you are being asked to do can be overwhelming at times. And you will need to be accurate and rigorous. Showing a bit of creativity is also a big plus and helps find solutions for each and every client.

What tools do you use most?

Marine: Jira and Trello for project management. Google Analytics, InVision, Photoshop or Sketch to design mock-ups. Salesforce, Zendesk, Usertesting; Mailjet and Mailchimp for emails.

#8 Pre-sales Manager

"No academic background is actually necessary because every product is different and you are going to have to learn its core specificities every time."

John Knipper, Gracenote

The pre-sales manager is a profile somewhere between a product specialist, a strategist and a salesperson working in support of the sales teams.

This position is typically found in companies selling products that require a good technical knowledge, as is the case for software publishers. This involves working with the sales team on the approach strategy and RFQs (Request For Quotation) or RFPs (Request For Proposal). The contribution of this person is crucial for convincing the customer that the product is the one best suited for their needs.

The duties of the position are clearly defined in medium and large-sized companies. In smaller companies, such as start-ups, this position frequently still needs to be defined, somewhere between the salesperson and the product manager and acting as support for the sales team. This can be carried out by anyone with a sales profile who understands the product or having a technical profile whilst being able to work with sales.

John Knipper
Title: Solution architect
Company: Gracenote
City: Berlin
Age: 43

What is a Solution Architect?

John: I often give myself the title of Solution Engineer or Sales Engineer. And I believe that in the United States this job is not seen in the same way as it is in Europe. I am simply the main technical contact for our clients: I explain how our product works, train, run benchmarks and organize events such as hackathons.

What education is required to be in that job?

John: No academic background is actually necessary because every product is different and you are going to have to learn its core specificities every time. Of course, it does require some technical skills like basic programming. But overall, it is experience that counts rather than what degree you hold.

What is the future of this job?

John: I see two possible paths. You can either become product manager because, as you spend so much time with clients, you see where the market is headed. The alternative is to go for a more tech job such as director of technical development. And as development costs have become so high in the US, a lot of these companies open tech offices in Europe so there will certainly be opportunities.

Brandon DeLap
Title: Senior pre-sales engineer
Company: Catchpoint
City: Los Angeles
Age: 28

Can you please describe your job?

Brandon: Pre-sales engineers at Catchpoint are the backbone to establishing value prior to and after onboarding a client. Pre-sales engineers articulate technology and functionality to the business owners and technical users. It's imperative for pre-sales engineers to establish and maintain strong relationships throughout the sales cycle. This way we can identify and communicate any technical issues that arise.

What do you do on a day-to-day basis?

Brandon I participate in prospect discovery calls to help qualify leads, provide product demonstrations, collaborate with development and product management to continuously improve Catchpoint solutions, assist clients in account configuration, training and onboarding, maintain professional and technical knowledge by attending educational workshops.

How do you see it evolving?

Brandon: I can see a significant decrease in travel per month and a shift to a more virtual world, especially since COVID-19. My desired career evolution would be to eventually be in a leadership role, leading a team of engineers and managing them to understand how to maximize customer value and retention.

#9 Developer

"I discovered coding through the Programming Olympics in my school. It's important to start developing young."

Ruslan Bulatov, Noveo

A developer can cover a range of tasks, as do most of the jobs described in this book. A front-end programmer, whose job may sometimes be assimilated to that of UX designer, does not work with the same programming languages or methods as a back-end developer who might develop solutions for optimizing the processing of large volumes of data for instance.

Recruiters are finding it very difficult to meet the demand for developers due to the exponential use of technology in all fields of the economy. These profiles are highly sought after. In turn, the salaries for these jobs tend to be very high, in the hundreds of thousands of dollars per year in the Silicon Valley in the more exceptional cases.

One should bear in mind the fact that most developers are not generally salary driven, at least not for the first 10 years of their careers and are probably the profile who are the least driven by money. What matters to developers are programming languages they train and work on. What we find is that their holy grail is to be able to work on the newest exciting tech project.

Most of the developer profiles come from IT or engineering backgrounds. Given the attractiveness of the job, shorter training and more accessible courses for non-tech profiles have appeared in the last 5 years.

For this reason the lines have become more blurred in terms of training and business school graduates now follow training courses in programming in order to acquire the basics in coding – and though they will never attain the same level as a confirmed developer who has trained on a confirmed language, that is not their ultimate aim.

Arun Ravuri
Title: Senior developer
Company: EditPlace India
City: Bangalore
Age: 31

What are you doing as a developer?

Arun: I manage the team of developers of EditPlace in India. EditPlace is a digital content solution for businesses. My role is to lead the team of local developers and deliver the product roadmap of the company.

What is your expertise and what technology do you use?

Arun: The tools that we use the most are: Zend/Laravel, Git, and Linux/GCP. I would say we need good problem-solving skills as I spend a good part of my time helping other team members fix issues.

How would you train someone new in your team?

Arun: We do start by having them work on small tasks. That is a period when I spend a lot of time with the newcomer and this allows me to know how s/he might react and whether s/he identifies mistakes. As the work progresses, we give them pre-defined objectives to achieve. However, every individual is different and we need to be flexible and adapt every time.

Ruslan Bulatov
Title: Senior Java developer
Company: Noveo
City: Saint Petersburg
Age: 32

How did you become a developer?

Ruslan: I have a Master's degree in applied mathematics and IT but I started programming when I was in school. I discovered coding through the Programming Olympics in my school. It's important to start developing young. The programming language or technology you use doesn't really matter.

What is your job?

Ruslan: I'm a back-end developer. My work is to build API (Application Programming Interface), REST (Representational State Transfer), back-end and database architectures. The goal of our team is to build stable and feature-rich applications. We write and review code, test and setup the CIS (Continuous Integration Server).

Where do you see yourself in 5 years?

Ruslan: I see two potential future paths for developers: become a team manager or go into project management. But I love programming and would like to keep writing code so my goal is to become a team manager and, down the line, CTO (chief technical officer).

Olivier Meyer
Title: UX front-end specialist
Company: Adobe
City: Paris
Age: 43

What do you do and what team are you in?

Olivier. I work in the UX team. I act as the UX support arm for all internal stakeholders such as Sales, Legal and other business units. We are also here to spread design thinking methods.

Can you describe a typical day?

Olivier. I design mock-ups and prototypes in compliance with the company's standard templates for almost half of the week. I also build user-friendly applications and ensure that the code we write and the architecture are of high quality and scalable.

What advice would you give for someone new at this job?

Olivier. Get inspiration where you can find it, including from outside companies. Especially those with a strong design culture like Apple, Google, Ideo or web agencies. Read a lot of UX and front-end articles. Be proactive and test new frameworks, experiment ideas in your personal folder.

#10 Strategic Planner

"Think as a beginner, act like a professional and keep in mind the fact that the world is always changing."

Daniel Kwintner, Sopexa

There are 2 main types of planners:

- The strategic planner usually works in an agency or for a brand and defines the global strategy of the brand or a given campaign. S/he needs to keep up with the times and societal trends and may specialize in one particular industry.

- The media planner defines the paid campaign strategy (paid media: advertising, sponsored content, etc.) on the various channels (display, Google, social media, etc.). The function involves defining the budgets allocated to each platform, the timing of communication and the intensity of the message.

Generally speaking, the role draws on a number of different studies such as market studies and the penetration of the media, in order to make the recommendations necessary to reach the target audience. It is the link between customers, the creation of formats and messages, and distribution.

On the media side, the purchase of digital advertising has been growing steadily in recent years and now exceeds purchases on more traditional platforms of TV, radio and newspapers in some countries. The automation of digital and programmatic advertising buying has given rise to a new term: traders. Traders buy advertising slots on private or public market places, transacting through auctions or with fixed rates, and fine-tune activity according to performance. Programmatic ad buying represents almost 70% of volumes in the most mature markets such as the United Kingdom and the United States and has become the default purchasing method for display digital advertising.

Media planners also act as negotiators - buying at the best price - and brand consultants. This job is found in media agencies, within trading desks concerning traders, as well as in large publishers.

Media planners generally come from advertising, communications or business backgrounds. The strategic planner is a senior level job and operational functions are limited, with more focus on the analysis and advisory role.

Guillaume Martin
Title: Head of strategy
Company: BETC (Havas)
City: Paris
Age: 42

What is your job at the agency?

Guillaume: Agencies provide creative input for the brands, to increase awareness of the brand and to help it move forward. Strategic planners make sure one finds the best messages that stick to the identity the brand develops. It has to make sense to consumers in a world where 75% of all brands could disappear tomorrow without anybody caring.

What is a typical day in the office?

Guillaume: I listen and challenge our clients' briefs, research to better meet their needs and identify the most relevant propositions. I write internal briefs for our creative team and explain our work to our clients.

Where is the position headed and what is your ambition?

Guillaume: I could not even tell you what I will be working on tomorrow. That is why I do what I do. That said, we are quickly moving away from the isolated planner that finds THE idea alone in his office. Planners nowadays must consider user experience as well as brand values. That means working closer with data and UX people - profiles that agencies now are very keen to recruit.

Federico Mancin
Title: Head of strategy
Company: The Big Now (Dentsu)
City: Milan
Age: 34

Can you describe the job of a strategic planner?

Federico: I like to think about a strategist as a sort of guardian angel for brands. The strategist gets briefs from clients and understands what the client needs. He has a strong knowledge of consumers and markets and then defines a strategy.

What qualities do you need in this job?

Federico: Analytical skills in order to process a vast amount of data, the ability to synthesize, as well as some good research skills to find the most relevant insights.

What is the future of your job?

Federico: I think the future of strategy and planning in the digital sector is all about measurability. There will be no differences between a strategist and consultant. The next big challenge will be to help brands and companies understand and prioritize KPIs. Data and technologies will be crucial but they will always need a human brain able to connect the dots.

Lesly Couty
Title: Senior strategic planner
Company: Ogilvy
City: Frankfurt
Age: 35

What is the purpose of your department?

Lesly: The main objective of a planning department is to help brands grow from a business and image perspective through a strong understanding of consumer behavior and then build the best possible customer experience. It can happen through a communication campaign, a CRM program or the launch of a new product or service.

What are your daily tasks? Who do you work with?

Lesly: I analyze a lot of consumer research, competitive landscapes and market trends. I build strategic recommendations before showing them to our clients. I write creative briefs and follow-up on the creative development phases. In order to do this, I need to use research portals, strategic frameworks or presentation tools such as Keynote or PowerPoint. I work closely with the project management teams when we define the clients' needs, plan and estimate a budget for the project. I stay involved in the creative process to make sure it is well executed and I report results afterwards.

What is the ideal background of a planner?

Lesly: People in planning come from diverse educational and professional backgrounds: sociology, business administration, data science and obviously communication. Most of them have a Master's degree or more. I studied foreign languages and law at university and then global communication at ISCOM Paris. I did my internship at Publicis Paris. I first joined the new business unit working on pitches then moved to account management and finally landed in the strategy department. I would advise people to first join an agency where the strategic planning is well-established in order to learn from people with a strong expertise.

Daniel Kwintner
Title: Strategic planner
Company: Sopexa
City: Tokyo
Age: 42

Why did you become a planner?

Daniel: I didn't follow the usual academic path. I have been working for over 22 years in various industries but always in relation with design and branding. I benefited from a background in design management and entrepreneurship which allowed me to listen to and understand what people need and want.

What do you do on a day-to-day basis?

Daniel: I manage crises with clients, when they occur, and find solutions with my team. I also spend time on client negotiations, brainstorming sessions, strategic planning meetings and market trends monitoring.

How would you train someone new in your job?

Daniel: The best thing is to work on real projects with real data. Learning from your mistakes. My first advice is: think as a beginner, act like a professional and keep in mind the fact that the world is always changing.

David Honig: Recruiting in digital marketing

Davis Honig is the head of MarketSearch and has been recruiting digital marketing professionals in the United States for 20 years. Here is his vision of the Digital Marketing recruitment market.

Congratulations on all the work you've done to earn your advanced marketing degree. Now, you'll use everything you've learned, over every channel imaginable to reach your target audiences and measure how successfully your campaigns can deliver results.

Marketing is not about creating an eye-catching graphic anymore. Analytics, measurements, geo-targeting are all attributes that the marketer of today and of the future will need to have mastered upon delivery for whatever firm you wish to work for. What has changed in marketing over time is the way that effective marketers can pinpoint their exact audiences and have the ability to convert them into lifelong and loyal customers. Marketing candidates need to be proficient and experienced in using tools such as Hubspot, Marketo and Salesforce from the very first day on the job. They should all be positioned nicely on your resume and have real case studies of how you've used them in the past to develop outstanding marketing results.

The demand for marketing managers is trending up fast. Obviously, everything web-related is a major growth driver. Any changes in technology, consumer behavior and the economy can dramatically impact the skills and expertise that businesses are looking for in marketing professionals. To stay relevant and employable in a changing field, marketers should keep up to date with new advances in digital and sales technology, develop both creative and analytical skills and have some understanding of the technical skills involved in programming, app development or website coding.

Technology has impacted the way companies view their work force structures. This shift further drives CMOs (chief marketing officer) to re-strategize how they recruit talent and highlight the need to have superior teams in place to prepare for the future of digital marketing. This means they have higher expectations from their talent pool and won't accept anything less than the extraordinary. CMOs who want to be at the forefront of innovation and succeed in the age of elevated customer experiences must hire top marketers with cutting-edge skill sets.

Preparing for the future requires a commitment to lifelong learning. Marketers need to keep one step ahead all the time. Marketers who leave work excited about what they've accomplished and return the next day to beat the control are marketers who I want to be connected with throughout their careers. Regardless of your current position, you have the power to propel yourself forward and build an incredibly rewarding career. Have the passion to set the pace. Have the confidence to lead. Be the marketer that companies want to have leading their teams.

What's the best way to market yourself and land on that dream job? Remember, you are the product. You need to examine what characteristics, features and skills make you unique - and stand out among competing job searchers and in the eyes of employers. These special characteristics include work experience, leadership, professional memberships and, of course, your education and training. What is the one thing that makes you different from any other job seeker applying for the same job? What's your unique selling point? Always do your research on the company before an interview but if you cannot properly communicate these benefits to employers, you will not get the job.

Network with current and former co-workers, colleagues, professional meetings, placement offices, alumni, recruiters and almost any gathering of people. How strong is your network? How can you make your network stronger? Always be marketing yourself. Not selling yourself, but instead, be strategically positioned in the marketing community. You want to be seen as a leader, an innovator and someone who has the ideas that people want to listen to and emulate. Employers seek marketers who aren't only attentive to changes that occur but those who embrace changes to heighten and leverage the opportunities that come with them. When you're interviewing for a job, think about sharing a situation in your career where you had to quickly adjust to a sudden change in the middle of a project and how you dealt with it to produce results.

Marketers need to be skilled at crunching data to identify opportunities and make the best possible decisions. While being number-oriented is important, marketers also need to come up with cool ideas that strike a chord with potential customers. Skills in analytics and empathy will be equally important in landing this role. Analytics will help you understand the data behind customer behaviors and empathy will give you the tools you need to communicate in ways that resonate with others and drive the desired behavior.

CMOs know all the disruptions have been unleashed by the digital and customer experience revolutions and it's here to stay. The fact that customers have more knowledge, expectations and power than ever before is a given. Today's connected customers are in control. They determine when/where/how they interact with your firm, and marketing must now follow its customers wherever they happen to be. CMOs understand their business's future is tied to its ability to respond in environments defined by complexity, speed and innovation.

The digital world won't wait for anyone, and marketers will have to take a proactive part in staying relevant and navigating through the rise of technology. Marketing professionals must continue to learn, adapt and develop new skills to set themselves as leading candidates.

This is undeniably important in the marketing space, where nothing is ever stagnant. Marketers must keep up to stay relevant. One must be able to adapt to changes in dynamically-driven industries. Marketers must demonstrate that they're staying ahead of trends through their own active learning. Employers don't just want to hear that you possess the ability to learn; they expect you to prove it.

Basically, think big, think cutting-edge, break through the work that will be noticed and admired by your industry. The game we were taught to play is no longer bound by the same rules. The rules have changed before but they've never changed like this. Most importantly have fun, love what you do and constantly continue learning. If you don't do this, you'll soon be replaced!

#11 Graphic Designer

"When you think something needs to be different, do it and show them why it is better."

Anouk Szabo, ASUS

The graphic designer is responsible for producing visuals.

Mastering vector graphic techniques and specific software packages, such as InDesign, is the way graphic designers best express their creativity. Each graphic designer has his/her own personal touch but must also be able to respond to needs, understand communication objectives and to translate them into the identity of brands and products.

Technical training in graphic design is essential but the end-products allow a designer to progress to other positions. This role is often found in agencies but many designers operate as freelancers after a few years of experience.

Whether as a graphic artist, in the strict sense, or an artistic director, in the case of more senior roles, there are a number of opportunities open to a graphic designer depending on his/her training and level of experience.

A designer may aspire to be an artistic or creative director, which is more focused on visual concepts than execution. In some cases, an artistic director can have a more junior profile without having been trained in design. In other cases, to have worked as a designer is a prerequisite for more creative positions or more senior level jobs.

This is a constantly evolving profession and a graphic designer needs to remain at the cutting edge of new creative techniques, technological innovations and the changes in consumer behavior on digital platforms.

Cristina Adonizio
Title: Art director
Company: Freelance
City: Rome
Age: 37

What education would you recommend in order to become a designer?

Cristina: Attending a design school is a must. You can work on different types of graphic jobs and learn to work on a number of tools which provide a good foundation of experience. I would also recommend you pick a specialization by following a Master's course. Going abroad for the most adventurous: it pushes you to learn other ways of working - and there are many of these in the graphic design world. In our job, it is crucial to master tools and find one's own way of working.

How does a typical day look?

Cristina: More interestingly, I can explain how a project develops. Step 1: plan, read the client brief, quote a number of days. Step 2: start researching, find examples such as images or creatives. Step 3: develop a concept. Step 4: create graphical examples. Step 5: execute.

Some advice for those who want to become an art director?

Cristina: In order to become AD, you need at least 3 years of experience in an agency. You first need experience in graphic design. Being an AD also means managing your time in order to deliver a project on time. This means scheduling each project step and trying to understand what potential issues you will have to work through.

Aurélien Foutoyet
Title: Web designer
Company: Freelance
City: Paris
Age: 37

As a freelance web designer who do you interact with the most?

Aurélien: It varies with each project. When I work with start-ups I talk to the leaders; with agencies, I talk to project managers. With a brand it can be the project, IT or digital manager.

What are the top 3 tools to master?

Aurélien: Creative softwares such as Sketch, Photoshop or Illustrator and prototyping tools such as InVision. And emails!

Do you see trends for the near future?

Aurélien: Digital jobs tend to be more and more specialized with experts at every step of the project: user experience manager, creative designer, motion designer, Unicorn developer. And we have access to more and more powerful tools such as animation prototyping software for motion design. We can be quicker and more efficient. This will accelerate over time.

Anouk Szabo
Title: Graphic designer
Company: ASUS
City: Amsterdam
Age: 25

What do you do for ASUS?

Anouk: I design campaigns, banners, flyers, point-of-sale communications material, websites as well as newsletters.

What advice would you give to a junior?

Anouk: Dare to do what you think is best. When you are just starting out, you can get stuck in doing exactly and only what's asked from you. So, when you think something needs to be different, do it and show them why it is better.

How do you see this job changing in the future?

Anouk: There are so many different types of designers right now: visual, graphic, digital designers… I think they are going to all merge in the future. Personally, I now work for a brand after having spent time in agencies and I would love to continue working on the client side.

#12 Content Producer

"Generation Z will change the way we talk and the new audience, the digital natives, will definitely be more demanding."

Giovanna Gallo, Freelance

The content producer emerged along with the advent of brand content - the messages and stories that companies want to get across to their audiences - beyond basic advertising formats. The decline in the impact of purely advertising messages has prompted brands to stand out for the quality and uniqueness of the content they produce and offer.

The content producer is now a specific role which was previously found in the functions of community managers and website managers.

Even if writing first springs to mind, it is video content that generates most engagement and is best adapted to current consumer habits. Audio formats such as podcasts that were previously ignored have now found a major audience among the urban youth and will soon penetrate more segments of society.

Coming from a background in communication, broadcasting or journalism, a content producer can work for a company within the framework of a long-term strategy, allowing one to work for the brand on a regular basis. Some specific tasks that require a specialized expertise that is not available internally will need to be provided by an agency or freelancer. However, as strategies and formats gain in maturity, brands are increasingly taking on these functions.

Giovanna Gallo
Title: Content producer
Company: Freelance
City: Turin
Age: 33

Which clients do you work for?

Giovanna: I mostly write for Cosmopolitan and Lonely Planet that are owned by Hearst Media. I also write for corporate websites and blogs.

How do you operate with your clients?

Giovanna: I work a lot from home but I choose topics with the brand's digital coordinator or communications manager. When I write an article, I must follow some rules: SEO but also the tone of voice and language that the brand develops.

How is this job going to evolve?

Giovanna: Generation Z will change the way we talk and the new audience, the digital natives, will definitely be more demanding.

Omran Omaid
Title: Content producer
Company: Shopify
City: Toronto
Age: 27

Can you tell us about your experience as a Content Producer?

Omran: I studied Design, Media as well as Film and TV production. I got an internship and the opportunity to shoot interviews with the likes of Phil Knight (Nike C.E.O.), Ronda Rousey and some other Olympic medallists. Then I got a job for a live streaming platform but I was also working on my own film projects, which helped me get the job I have now.

What do you do all day?

Omran: I spend most of my time crafting ideas and stories: pre-production, storyboarding, filming interviews and video editing for internal broadcasting. I use the Adobe Creative Suite, mainly Premiere Pro and After effects, filming equipment (light, lenses, camera) and some project planning tools such as Google calendar, Asana and Trello.

What advice would you give to someone starting in the industry?

Omran: At Shopify, they hire you for a reason. They know you are good at what you do, so be confident in yourself. Learn about the company you are working for, understand the culture, the values, the people as much as possible. And you will get better naturally.

Francesca Nicasio
Title: Content marketing manager
Company: Vend
City: Los Angeles
Age: 32

How did you land in content production?

Francesca: I have a degree in Business Communication. I always loved writing and was a correspondent for my university's school paper. After graduation, I took on writing jobs and became a freelance writer. That was when I started learning about blogging, WordPress, SEO, content marketing.

Can you describe your job for us?

Francesca: I look after all our content marketing efforts at Vend, a retail management software. It includes our blog as well as resources such as eBooks, whitepapers and reports. My objective is to drive traffic, awareness and leads through content. A secondary objective is to increase Vend's authority in the retail space: through the distribution of relevant content, people are more likely to see Vend as a leader in the industry. About half of my time is spent on content production: writing articles, conducting interviews, conducting research, formatting and publishing. Another third is about thinking about what to publish next, looking for relevant keywords and assigning content pieces to other writers.

Who do you interact the most with?

Francesca: I report to the Head of digital marketing. I work with people that look after paid acquisition and distribute our content - through Google and Facebook ads. As for organic traffic growth, I work with our SEO folks. If the product or regional marketers launch a new feature or run a regional campaign, I would also support them with relevant content.

#13 Acquisition Manager

"The online marketing world is constantly changing. Search engine marketing and channels that I was working on 6 years ago are no longer the same."

Cristina Padilla, Babbel

The job of acquisition manager has become much more important in the last few years due to the growth of online business and SaaS.

The main objective of this job is to optimize the traffic generated and the number of conversions on the brands' websites and mobile applications. This is done by conceiving, configuring and managing advertising campaigns on the various platforms through which an audience may be captured such as Google, social networks, other websites and mobile store apps.

E-commerce websites also use affiliate systems. Some acquisition managers may also be responsible for SEO and will need to master search engines in order to index the website content.

To date, this position is typically found in specialized web agencies that work with SME (Small and Medium-sized Enterprise) clients or with some larger accounts. A growing number of large companies now have an internal department within their digital marketing departments.

A background in web marketing or advertising is helfpful in order to become an acquisition manager. A background in communication will open more doors when content is key and the job is coupled with that of SEO Manager.

Cristina Padilla
Title: Senior SEM manager
Company: Babbel
City: Berlin
Age: 33

Can you please explain your job?

Cristina: My job is to ensure that the right user sees and interacts with our ads at the right moment and in the right context. My job combines a strategic part (define and execute channel strategy, tactics and roll-outs for certain countries) with operations (planning, forecasting, reporting and coordination of media campaigns).

What tools do you use the most?

Cristina: Google/Bing/Apple Ads, Excel or Data Studio and all analytical and test tools (Google Analytics, Outfit, Visual Website Optimiser, Adjust, Amplitude).

What are the biggest changes currently happening in your field?

Cristina: The online marketing world is constantly changing. Search engine marketing and channels that I was working on 6 years ago are no longer the same. In SEM, everything is becoming more automated. And there will be new channels coming up in the near future, similar to what I have been experiencing so far. I think this is a great opportunity for every marketer to grow professionally.

Andrea Gonzalez
Title: Digital campaign manager
Company: Go-to Skincare
City: Sydney
Age: 29

Can you please explain your job?

Andrea: I look after all digital marketing campaigns, from search to paid social, display, retargeting, emailing and website optimization. I manage our digital budget and develop our digital marketing strategy. I brief the creative team about all required assets and developers if necessary. I work with 3 external agencies depending on campaigns. Part of my role is also analytical with reports on campaigns and customer behavior analysis.

What qualities are required for that job?

Andrea: Good time management is critical. You need to be able to work with different teams and be adaptable, especially in a small organization.

How do you see your job moving forward?

Andrea: The best thing about a digital marketing job is that it is constantly changing and evolving. No one really knows how it will be in 5 years. No one could have predicted paid social media would become so important 5 years ago. Will influencers still be big in 5 years' time? It's really hard to tell and that's why it's so important to keep learning and follow industry news.

Mirela Cialai
Title: Director of mobile marketing
Company: Zinio
City: New York City
Age: 45

Can you please describe your job?

Mirela: Zinio (Naviga group) is an online newsstand that converts print magazines to digital content. I work with our mobile team to drive brand awareness and subscriber growth. To do so we develop our overall marketing strategy, oversee ideation and execution of initiatives and top-of-funnel campaigns. Our KPIs are related to the app customer behavior. We focus on how customers interact with our marketing content.

How do you spend your days?

Mirela: I analyze in-app consumer behavior and retention rate of new users, prepare weekly performance reports and share them with the leadership team. I identify issues and craft strategies to address those issues, look for opportunities to reach new markets and grow our user base as well as monitor competition.

What was your background before joining Zinio?

Mirela: I have a BA in Economics and more than 15 years of B2C (business-to-consumer) experience leading global digital strategies, always in a multinational environment. My expertise is about brand awareness, digital and mobile innovation.

#14 Recruiter

"Develop thick skin – this job will knock you back every day so you need to be able to get up and go again."

Nathan Davies, Marketing Moves

We chose to place the job of recruiter within the job matrix because all the actors of this field need, at some point or other, to call upon the services of a recruitment agency or to use a recruiting manager in their own company. The scarcity of qualified profiles in some jobs in the digital sector have made this function crucial. A recruiter's role is, and will continue to be, to find the right candidate. This role is even harder in the digital field but also more interesting due to 4 main factors.

Firstly, it is a young activity, which emerged some 20 years ago and within which new jobs appear every 18 to 24 months. The positions of digital scientist or growth marketer are just two of the most recent examples.

Secondly, the educational system needs to adapt and produce training and profiles that answer to shifting business needs. This of course takes time and as a consequence there is often a lack of good candidates for some of the functions listed in the matrix.

The recruiter is also not immune to the platform phenomenon which has impacted other activities. The role has become more structured in recent years and now comprises a number of specialized actors. Over the past three years, we have seen the emergence of specialized actors, such as ZipRecruiter in the United States or Malt.fr in France.

Some of these platforms are more than just simple linking tools. They also incorporate personality analysis algorithms (such as Applied) or advanced video resume tools (Tempo) – both of which are British start-ups.

Lastly, the sector is at the forefront of the freelance movement. A large number of the positions we have listed (graphic designers, community managers or developers) are filled by freelancers. As a consequence, this is having an impact on the recruiting process, on budgets and on the relationship between the company and the person performing the job.

Nathan Davies
Title: Managing partner
Company: Marketing Moves
City: London
Age: 42

Can you describe your job for us?

Nathan: I see myself as a 360-degree recruiter who serves his clients. My job is going out into the wider market to source, headhunt and attract the perfect candidate for a job my client is hiring for. To be successful in recruitment you have to know your market and hiding behind a phone or email will not deliver the best experience for either client or candidate

What does it require?

Nathan: You cannot be in this job if you do not truly like to meet people. So being open is a requirement. And to develop thick skin – this job will knock you back every day so you need to be able to get up and go again

What will the role of a recruiter be in 2025?

Nathan: I think the industry will become more and more reliant on technology, where automation and A.I. begin to take over the daily tasks associated with the role. However, nothing will replicate the human touch, meeting people face-to-face and networking on a personal and social level, which is why there will always be a place for a good recruiter!

James Pounder
Title: Digital recruiter
Company: Michael Page
City: Tokyo
Age: 32

What is your profile and job at Michael Page?

James: I studied history at Columbia University in New York City. After an internship as an English teacher in Tokyo, I started to work for Michael Page. My job is to develop commercial relationships with companies operating in Japan in the digital and online industry (multinational e-commerce companies, social networking firms, app-based businesses, etc.). I source both local and international talents such as digital marketers, e-commerce specialists, software engineers or data scientists.

How do you measure success? How do you get there?

James: Our mission is to achieve monthly revenue and productivity targets but we also have a number of strategic objectives such as developing a specific industry for instance. For that matter, you need to have a deep understanding of the recruitment process, negotiation skills and good networking skills so that you can establish and nurture meaningful relationships.

Will it still be the same job in 10 years?

James: The role of a recruiter will undoubtedly become more and more impacted by technology. How recruiters search and interact with candidates will become increasingly reliant on recommendation systems, CRM (customer relationship management) tools and the likes. Additionally, the types of positions that recruiters support may change drastically in the long term because positions related to artificial intelligence, machine learning and engineers are likely to become more prominent.

Christine Metaillier
Title: Talent advocate
Company: Talent.io
City: Paris
Age: 32

Can you tell what Talent.io is and describe your job?

Christine: Talent.io is a recruitment platform for all types of profiles in the digital world. Our ambition is to become the leader in Europe. I spend most of my time searching for new candidates, interviewing them, writing reports and coaching.

What does it take to be a Talent Advocate?

Christine: To be curious, driven but also show some patience and resilience. It is a sales job and it often requires you to be able to step back and analyze.

Is there an ideal education or degree to become one?

Christine: It of course depends on your profile but the most popular degrees to get here are business schools or degrees in Human Resources and Psychology.

Élise de Saint Didier
Title: Founder
Company: Executive Search Digital
City: Los Angeles
Age: 40

Can you tell us more about ESD and your role?

Élise: Executive Search Digital is a recruitment agency in the digital space that I created and which is based in Los Angeles. My job is to identify and recruit the best talents, often for director roles for retails groups and tech start-ups.

Why did you create your own agency?

Élise: You do not become a recruiter fresh out of school. You build your career and develop your expertise and network over time. I came to recruitment as I had to find the best candidates for clients and I then decided to launch my own business.

What will a recruiter look like in 2025?

Élise: Sourcing is becoming more automated. That being said, if it was already all automated our clients would go on LinkedIn and Indeed to recruit directly. Only 2% of resumes sourced from platforms are a good match. So, it might not be that easy to do it all through machines and algorithms.

#15 Investor

"When it comes to tools, PowerPoint, email and a phone is all you need!"

Virginie Lazès

It seemed essential to include the role of investor as it has a central role in the digital ecosystem. Under this heading, we have grouped 2 jobs within the sector: organizations that invest in start-ups such as Venture Capitalists, as well as those that provide mergers and acquisitions consulting services.

The main categories of investors within the start-up ecosystem are as follows:

- Love Money is the term for persons close to the entrepreneurs, such as family and friends, who invest at the project's inception, often relatively small amounts.

- The BA (Business Angels or Angels) generally invest amounts in the hundreds of thousands of dollars during the first 12 to 18 months of the project.

- The VCs (Venture Capitalists) may invest a few million dollars for the initial financing (series A), a few tens of millions (series B) or 50 million or more (series C).

It is therefore possible for an investor to work in one or other of these fund types either as an analyst or partner depending on seniority level. The job of the analyst will be to work upstream on the screening of future potential investments and assessing the feasibility of deals, and downstream on investment management.

The role of the venture capitalist is, more generally, to identify young and promising investment opportunities who will invest wisely and report the projected yield over a given period - generally 5 to 10 years depending on the profile of the fund.

The position requires a solid knowledge of the market and of emerging actors. This involves constantly meeting with as many entrepreneurs as possible.

Interestingly, for the past few years, corporates have also been creating investment funds in order to not miss out on the next upcoming start-up which may revolutionize the market. It is also possible to work as an analyst within these structures.

Vinoth Jayakumar
Title: Venture capitalist
Company: Draper Esprit
City: London
Age: 35

What is your role at Draper?

Vinoth: I am a venture capitalist. The job consists in finding companies in which we can invest and manage our existing investment portfolio. You need to constantly meet entrepreneurs, interview people and make some research to raise funds.

What tools do you use?

Vinoth: I use common tools such as the Google or Microsoft suites but also some sourcing tools such as Crunchbase to find the best start-ups.

What is the future of your business?

Vinoth: There are always emerging technologies. Mobile was the big thing 10 years ago and now everything is about artificial intelligence. I also see that the way we exchange with stakeholders is always more digital and relations are going to become overall more decentralized.

Virginie Lazès
Title: Partner
Company: NC
City: Paris
Age: 50

What is your job?

Virginie: I lead an M&A bank that focuses on new technologies. My mission is to sell tech companies to industry or financial groups. I spend 50% of my time with our team and the other 50% with clients.

What skills does it require?

Virginie: Hard skills required are a strong basis in finance, i.e. knowing how to read a balance sheet, structure a deal or value a business, and all of it in English. Soft skills are also crucial: interpersonal and mediation skills with your clients. When it comes to tools, PowerPoint, email and a phone is all you need!

What do you see happening in the next 5 years?

Virginie: Technology, starting with IA and deep learning, is going to spread across all sectors. It is a good thing as our playground is going to get far larger but also a risk as we will soon vie against competitors that were not looking at technology before.

Alex Lazarow
Title: Investment director
Company: Cathay Capital
City: San Francisco
Age: 35

Can you explain what Cathay Capital and you do?

Alex: I am an investment director at Cathay Capital, a fund that invests between $5 million and $20 million in every company we decide to support. I can categorize my work with these 5 tasks: I source companies where we can invest, set-up the deals, help our existing investments, also raise money for the fund and work on some of the fund operations.

What trends do you see in venture capitalism?

Alex: Our job is constantly evolving. We are seeing new models and new players emerge (and sometimes disappear) all the time: micro-funds, mega-funds (that of Softbank is the best example) or corporate ventures that nowadays account for over half of the deals (in value) in the US.

What does it take to be a good VC?

Alex: First and foremost, develop a good balance between analytical capacity and humility. I also think a fund might not be the place for junior profiles to start out in, as in our world you need to be efficient from day one.

Carolina Milanesi: Technology and education

Carolina Milanesi is the founder of Heart of Tech, a consumer technology consulting company. Carolina is a well-known figure in the Edtech and diversity fields. She has outlined for us her vision of how education is being transformed through technology. Carolina lives in the heart of the Silicon Valley and is an advocate of homeschooling.

Schools are meant to develop skills and capabilities while encouraging kids to "*think differently*" and maximize their abilities. Sadly, most schools are failing to do so today. The reasons rest within curricula that are not keeping up with the pace of change our world is undergoing, teachers set in their ways with little support to embrace change and technology thrown in for good measure often without a clear purpose. In other words, schools continue to operate on the basis of fulfilling the needs of an Industrial Age student rather than preparing students for the Information Age. Some say the entrenched teacher-centered methods have become a hybrid that incorporates a student-centered approach. While this is true, the change towards this hybrid approach might relate more to the need to deal with a larger number of students in one class than a real change towards fostering collaboration and critical thinking among students.

Technology: Friend or Foe?

One cannot talk about how education is changing without assessing the role technology should have in the classroom. Some, such as the parents who act as facilitators for empowering children (especially in K-12) with knowledge, blame technology. Apparently, having kids learn through apps puts teachers at a disadvantage in the classroom because they are now faced with students who show different levels of knowledge and skills. It also puts pressure on teachers to rely more on technology, not something many necessarily feel comfortable with. The big difference today is it's not just about acquiring knowledge. It is about learning in a different way which puts pressure on teachers. Pressure to relate to children in a different way. The same pressure many employers are facing as Millennials, and Gen Z after them, join the work force. The main reason why technology creates a challenge is that schools are focused on standardization, not customization. From teaching to tests, schools today are about students fitting a mold and falling within predetermined parameters that leave little room for individuality, let alone creativity and critical thinking.

Adding Devices is not the Same as Integrating Technology

Children are learning in a very different way today. Children who have access to technology and games such as Minecraft learn a new kind of creativity, one that has no physical limits. If you spend a few minutes talking to a Minecraft-obsessed child (like mine), you can see these pixelated worlds teach them about different materials, food, resource management, project planning, teamwork (if they use the multiplayer mode), problem-solving, responsibility and accountability for their animals. A whole host of YouTube programs - like Mineflix - are also teaching kids how they can learn and express themselves through storytelling which plays a huge role in modern gaming. Children learn more about their world and their building options and try them out themselves. The virtual manipulation Minecraft allows is like Lego creativity on steroids. Microsoft created the Minecraft Education Edition and teachers who have used it speak of higher engagement, collaboration, experimentation and a greater sense of accomplishment. Embracing tools like Minecraft Education Edition can pivot the learning environment from teacher-centered to student-centered, where students not only teach other students but they can help teachers learn. These new methods can help the transition from a textbook-driven method to a research-driven one, from passive learning to active learning, from a fragmented curriculum to an integrated and interdisciplinary one, much like the skills the workplace will require.

The Holy Grail of Personalized Education

As artificial intelligence grows in importance for tech companies around the world, our education system should focus on giving our children the skills they need to have a successful career when they grow up. This starts with acknowledging the skill sets my generation were taught (and served me well) are no longer critical for my daughter. As we prepare our children to face a world where A.I. transforms the opportunities in the workplace there is a chance to leverage the same A.I. to improve our current education system. Schools have been treating kids as if they were all the same. Public schools, in particular, are given an academic plan for the year. A plan that dictates what the children must learn and at what pace as well as how they are tested. This does not favor children who might have learning styles that do not conform. Of course, the big challenge of the classroom is that you often have a ratio of one teacher to twenty or more students, which dramatically limits the level of personal attention these children get. This is precisely where technology can play a significant role in designing a curriculum that takes into account the different levels of abilities children might have and help them thrive within the class environment. OneNote's Live Caption functionality can help children learn a language that is not their first language as well as children who might be hard of hearing. Technology can also better bridge school and home, providing tools to parents to better support their children through accessing videos provided by teachers for children who might have missed classes or assistance with writing, reading and even learning presentation skills.

Widening the Borders of Learning

Teachers, like many IT managers, have also to face the fact that children have access to technology like never before. This means that they have access to a level of information like never before opening up both opportunities and challenges that technology can help exploit or contain. With so much knowledge that is just a search or a digital assistant question away, children need to understand where the information is coming from by learning how to quote correctly in their work. Microsoft provides the ability to check your work against plagiarism with Copyleaks, making sure that other people's work is appropriately credited. Google takes it one step further with Originality Reports as part of the Google Suite, which allows teachers to check students' work against other students' current or previous work. Learning to rely on other people's work to shape your own thinking and opinion and understanding the difference between that and just simply using other people's work is critical and something that will become more and more important as they get older.

Now think of the role that a tool like Microsoft Stream automatic captions and searchable transcripts with support for eight languages coupled with the power of Microsoft Translator can play in widening the pool of educators we can access. Either as a homeschooler educator or a parent who gets involved in their kids' homework, we can now look at educators in countries that are ahead of the United States in personalized teaching and use their material to help us get there. It is a reflection of the boundless world our kids already live in today. Do you think the fact that their favorite YouTuber or Twitch player is in another country and speaks a different language stops them from learning tricks that make them better at Fortnite? If you have a Gen Zer in your home, you know the answer is 'no', so why should it be different when it comes to learning about science or math? I look forward to seeing how A.I. can enable better thinking by helping surfacing data and information. It is not about having A.I. taking over the role of educators or doing the work of students but rather empowering both with more knowledge and a basic understanding so their thinking and their learning will get exponentially broader, more diverse and inclusive.

#16 UX Manager

"It brings strategy, design and technology development together."

Juraj Vojnik, BCG Digital Ventures

UX refers to user experience sometimes also referred to as UI for user interface.

Whether dealing with websites or software application interfaces, the role of the UX manager is to ensure a smooth navigation between the various sections so that users are able to find what they are looking for and for this to happen the architecture and structure of the website must be consistent.

Here are two examples of actors for whom this challenge is crucial:

- Online retailers, for whom navigation is a key element for the act of purchasing. One button placed in two different parts of the site can generate very different conversion rates. One of the main challenges is adapting interfaces for audiences with varying levels of aptitude with digital content and the different access modes (computer with a 16:9 landscape screen or smartphone in portrait mode) and differing connectivity (broadband, 3G or 4G network, Wi-Fi…).

- Software and applications developers, who tend to have a more and more mobile-first view and for whom it is important to ensure that the proposed tool will be easy to use. A customer who actually uses the tool will be more inclined to renew their license at the end of the contract.

The UX manager position is located in design teams and requires know-how of graphic tools such as Photoshop, InDesign, Sketch as well as digital design techniques. A UX manager also needs a good knowledge of marketing in order to identify the evolutions and needs of users. Monitoring technological evolutions is also essential as the industry changes rapidly (HTML5, CSS3…).

Entry-level positions are found mainly in communications and software development agencies. Some companies seek purely technical positions, which are more UX design oriented and require fewer interactions with other functions such as content producer, acquisition manager or CRM manager.

Juraj Vojnik
Title: Experience lead design
Company: BCG Digital Ventures
City: Los Angeles
Age: 40

What is BCG Digital Ventures?

Juraj: We are a start-up integrated in Boston Consulting Group whose mission is to invent, launch and scale businesses for the world's most influential corporations.

What is an experience lead design exactly?

Juraj: My job is to develop new products and services, taking into consideration the complexities of delivering business and customer values. It requires an immense attention to details and forward-thinking. Experience lead design brings strategy, design and technology development together.

What skills does this also require?

Juraj: I would say empathy, acceptance of criticism about user testing and team research. Being able to listen and accept feedback, including negative comments. And speed and flexibility.

Mischa Weiss-Lijn
Title: UX manager
Company: Google
City: London
Age: 44

What is your role at Google?

Mischa: I manage a design team that works on a suite of internal SRE (Site Reliability Engineering) apps for Google. The team includes eight product designers, three user researchers and one product manager. I manage the designers, drive our design processes and work with our management team.

What do you do on a daily basis?

Mischa: I have 1-one-1s with my team members. I also support, mentor and work through issues. I review design work, work on key projects and drive design process optimizations.

How is your function going to change?

Mischa: We are shifting away from designers specialized in UX and visual design towards 'Unicorn' product designers. We are moving from an industry dominated by design agencies towards one where we will have strong teams on the client side. Young designers will have the opportunity to gain experience in agencies. It also means that managers will need to have a broad skill set covering UX, research and visual design.

Debbie Yang
Title: UX manager
Company: SAP
City: Shanghai
Age: 39

What education and job experience do you have?

Debbie: I hold a master's degree in Human Computer Interaction. I started working as user experience designer, followed by user research work before being promoted to UX manager. Candidates usually have a rich experience in interaction design and user research. Some of them are also good in visual design. But education in human computer interaction, industrial design, product design, psychology or fine arts would also fit well.

What tools do you need to master?

Debbie: Microsoft Office, Axure, and Photoshop.

How will this job grow?

Debbie: Interaction design is changing as technologies are evolving. For example, conversational UI is playing a more important part now. UX managers always have to follow and acquire knowledge about new trends.

#17 Data Scientist

"It is important to not lose sight of the commercial benefits your work is supposed to bring."

Nicolò Musmeci, Aviva

In the digital world, everything can be traced and the amount of data collected is too vast to be managed manually or with tools such as Excel.

A data scientist is responsible for analyzing and making the data available in the most suitable format possible. This requires an excellent knowledge of data capture, storage, extraction and analysis methods. The data scientist will manage the database architecture in order to take into account the 5Vs of big data: volume, velocity, variety, veracity and value.

Depending on the needs of the company, the position may be geared more towards analytics (in particular for marketing purposes), forecasting (through statistical models or machine learning) or automation. The data analysts actually use the data, whereas data scientists bring a cross-level approach to assemble databases without necessarily providing a conclusion about the meaning or possible use of the data.

Proficiency in a number of languages is required – typically programming languages, such as Python, C++ or JavaScript, are used for the automatization of data ingestion, SQL for data extraction and R and SAS for data analysis. Positions in data science are mostly for IT graduates, whereas data analysts could have more of a marketing background.

Data scientists are among the most sought-after profiles in the digital marketing sector today as they combine both technical and marketing expertise and because the need for data management and use of the data is constantly growing. It is rare to find a role which is both technical and business-oriented in this way.

This knowledge of data processing can lead to other positions such as analyst, CRM manager or chief technology officer.

Thea Backlar
Title: Data scientist
Company: Ogury
City: Paris
Age: 33

Can you describe your role for us?

Thea: I work as a product manager for all insights at Ogury, a start-up in mobile marketing. I have two main objectives: developing new insight products and improving our existing products..

What did you do before this job?

Thea: I graduated from Columbia University in Psychology. I came into the advertising industry by chance as I was working in a company that specialized in ad research. I then went on to work at ComScore and then moved to Ogury as Director of Studies.

What is your day made up of?

Thea: Meetings take up about 90% of my time, either internal or with clients. I liaise with various teams, work on product planning, build proposals or investigate existing problems.

Nicolò Musmeci
Title: Senior data scientist
Company: Aviva
City: London
Age: 32

What did you study and how did you get to that position?

Nicolò: I have a PhD in Financial Mathematics and a Master in Physics. Before joining Aviva, I was a data scientist for a lending company. The inquisitive mindset of research that I learned during my PhD has definitely helped me be a better data scientist.

What is it like to be a data scientist at Aviva?

Nicolò: I support marketing in personalizing our communication campaigns through A/B testing, machine learning models and data visualization. My goal is to bring the latest techniques in order to create a better customer experience. Half of my time is dedicated to exploring and preparing data, 25% on data modelling and the rest on understanding business needs and requirements.

What makes a good data scientist?

Nicolò: One needs to be fluent in SQL, Python and R. I would say one also needs to be proactive in finding new opportunities for applying data science. Strong communication and presentation skills for non-technical audiences are a big plus. It is important to not lose sight of the commercial benefits your work is supposed to bring. I would add that NLP (Natural Language Processing) and image recognition will probably become more widespread, so the use of libraries like Keras or Fastai will become a necessary requirement for data scientists.

Pawel Goralczyk
Title: Senior data scientist
Company: Deliveroo
City: London
Age: 34

Can you describe your background?

Pawel: I have a Master in Applied Mathematics from Warsaw University and am interested in subjects around statistics. I initially worked for market research companies (Nielsen, GFK) as an analyst and then moved to London to join King (Candy Crush) as a data scientist on mobile games. I recently moved to Deliveroo.

What is your daily routine?

Pawel: I work on designing and analyzing experiments conducted across our food delivery network. I work closely with software engineers or other data scientists who implement machine learning models to improve delivery performance.

What will this job become?

Pawel: Many things can be automated and this is already becoming a big part of what I do. Experimentation will be more and more automated even if non-standard or sophisticated analyses will always require human input.

#18 SEO Manager

"*SEO is still in its infancy and breaking away from a shady past of deception and manipulation.*"

Jane Sanderson, DAC

Search Engine Optimization means improving the visibility of website content and mobile applications within search engines in order to increase organic, as opposed to paid, traffic.

90% of users who search on Google using a computer click on a link appearing on the first page of search results and 70% will click on the top three results. These figures are even higher on those using mobile phones, which are the main source of internet traffic. The job of SEO manager involves establishing an appropriate strategy between using the most competitive generic search terms and a long tail, where the least used keywords can make it easier to gain additional visibility.

An SEO is a multifaceted role which depends on content format, which can be either audio, video, text or interactive. The SEO manager increasingly works with new vertical search tools such as the Appstore, Amazon for online retailers and YouTube with video content.

With the constant evolution of algorithms, an SEO manager needs to constantly keep informed and adapt to updates. The role involves continuous contact with content producers, one of the pillars of indexation and with UX managers, graphic designers, as well as developers, regarding the quality of the platforms.

This position is at the crossroads between communication and digital technology. It requires a strong digital culture but not necessarily high-end technical skills. Knowledge of HTML, however, is a real asset.

Various backgrounds can lead to this position but the experience of an SEO is generally in communications, languages, journalism and digital marketing. In smaller structures, the role may be combined with that of content producer, SEA (Search Engine Advertising) or acquisition manager, UX manager and even community manager.

Jane Sanderson
Title: SEO manager
Company: DAC
City: Toronto
Age: 45

What is your background?

Jane: I have a BA in English and History but I also took a number of coding and psychology classes. I've worked on websites since I left university and I have been working in SEO for 7 years. Candidates who have a higher education, have caring skills (about clients) and who are hardworking tend to excel as SEO managers.

What quick training would you give to a newbie?

Jane: It depends on the personalities but I would provide them with a generic understanding of SEO including its history. I would describe the details of the work we do and the benefits for clients. I would also encourage them to research and learn on their own. I would walk them through specific tasks. This field is always changing and I suggest they learn to love learning.

How is this job going to change?

Jane: I can see SEO becoming specialized by industry, for example Auto, FMCG (Fast Moving Consumer Goods), e-commerce or by search engine (Amazon, Google, YouTube). SEO is still in its infancy and breaking away from a shady past of deception and manipulation. In the future, I expect SEO to expand its horizons to include topics such as web accessibility, internal site search, improving website quality and user experience.

Elissaveta Iankova
Title: Senior content marketing manager
Company: Zalando
City: Berlin
Age: 33

What are your objectives as a SEO manager?

Elissaveta: The aim is to be number one in all Google keywords relevant to our activity. We are a big team so we work really closely together.

What is your function and what tools do you use?

Elissaveta: I run performance reports and check the evolution of our rankings and that of our competitors. I also monitor the progress we are making on the projects we are working on. I mostly use Google products such as Google Analytics, Google Console and Google AdWords.

Where do you see yourself in the future?

Elissaveta: I will stay in marketing but not in SEO.

Aneel Badyal
Title: SEO manager
Company: Saatchi & Saatchi
City: Toronto
Age: 29

How do you train for SEO?

Aneel: A general background in marketing is good to have but SEO requires more on-field experience than theory, as most schools do not teach SEO. There are resources for training online with websites such as moz.com that offer guides for SEO beginners. You can train on Google's website for free on their products. I mostly use Google Search Console and Google My Business. One needs to grow one's content writing skills, research, reporting and analytical capabilities to develop a good SEO expertise.

What trends can you notice in your industry?

Aneel: Automation is going to gain importance. More education and training are going to be necessary as the digital marketing world keeps developing. The industry is also going to change due to the control from Google and the evolution of other search engines.

And how will you play your part?

Aneel: I will focus more on strategy and work less on implementation. I will work more with artificial intelligence and programs to make better decisions and standardize tasks. I will continue experiments and develop improvements based on results.

#19 Sales Manager

"I love the adrenaline shot when you're in the middle of negotiations with a client and you begin to realize that you're going to close the deal."

Patrick Amelson, Xperi

As in any sector, the role of the sales manager is to sell a product or service and in particular to grow their network.

In the digital field, perhaps more so than in any other position, a sales manager may encompass several types of jobs. In essence, there are two main roles:

- The new business manager, whose role is to seek out new clients. In the future, these profiles will have to work more closely with the marketing department, whose job is to provide contacts and leads created through online marketing.

- The account manager handles existing clients. S/he needs to spend more time with the project and product management teams, who ensure the smooth running of the project and client satisfaction.

The SDR (Sales Development Representative) is an emerging role which developed within software companies. It is a link between the digital marketing and sales teams, and filters and develops leads generated via digital contacts.

Most salespeople have attended business school or shorter vocational training programs. The role of the salesperson requires, above all else, open mindedness, emotional intelligence and good communication skills but also discipline and determination, which is too often underestimated. The qualities, methods and the frame of mind needed can vary according to the structure in which the salesperson works. S/he may have to rely on a personal network and his or her *intuiti personae*, whereas someone working for a software company or for a SaaS technology, most customer acquisition will happen online, using automated lead generation methods.

Jessica Lim
Title: Regional senior sales manager
Company: RTB House
City: Singapore
Age: 30

What is your role at RTB House?

Jessica: RTB House provides personalized advertising solutions and my role is to demonstrate the value of our products all the way through the sales cycle - from prospects to clients. I work with the sales teams to have top-notch sales processes, strategies and pitches.

How do you manage your time?

Jessica: Prospecting, managing our pipeline and forecasting sales take most of my time. We look at our sales pipeline and what to improve during weekly team meetings. I liaise internally with the client service team to track campaign performances. I also scan the industry news regularly.

How do you see your role in the future?

Jessica: I think sales jobs will be increasingly run through artificial intelligence and automation. I will probably be less into pure sales but more into operations or account management.

Ludovic Thevelin
Title: Account executive
Company: Google
City: New York City
Age: 27

Can you please describe your role and objectives?

Ludovic: I work in NYC for Google in a team of 6. We work with businesses that are new to our products (Google Marketing Solutions) and help them succeed in using them. I manage my own portfolio. Our objective is to drive growth for Google by attracting and sustaining the highest potential clients.

What do you concretely do on a daily basis?

Ludovic: I spend a lot of time on growing clients. 30% of my time is spent through client-facing meetings, 25% in reviewing accounts and performance and 25% in conducting research and defining strategies. The rest is spent on admin tasks or various projects. It requires good sales, time-management and problem-solving skills.

Where do you see yourself in a few years' time?

Ludovic: The job is becoming more about building sustainable relations with clients rather than one-off advertising campaigns. I see myself move towards strategy and design rather than core product-related jobs. We're moving towards a lot of automation and deep product knowledge in advertising is becoming less useful.

Patrick Amelson
Title: Regional sales manager
Company: Xperi
City: Munich
Age: 45

Can you tell us what Xperi is and what you do there?

Patrick: I am an international sales manager at Xperi which is a tech leader in audio solutions. I run the auto vertical: my clients are car makers and automotive suppliers for sound system, radio or driver monitoring system.

What makes your job specific?

Patrick: I sell tech products and therefore have to rely on internal product experts such as our pre-sales guys. They come and meet clients with me. The other important thing to understand is that we work through relatively long sales cycles that follow new vehicle launches - between 5 to 8 years. Each and every salesperson in the company therefore only looks after a handful of large clients.

What do you enjoy most?

Patrick: I love the adrenaline shot when you're in the middle of negotiations with a client and you begin to realize that you're going to close the deal. I also appreciate the way we operate at Xperi: it is a California-based company and people work from a lot of different areas across the globe, mostly from home. I travel a lot (before COVID-19 happened) even if video calls help a lot. One more thing is that our bonuses are mostly based on company performances instead of individuals goals. It is because it requires several salespeople to work on the same global account - one for BMW Europe, one for BMW in the United States for instance. It is complicated to attribute bonuses on an individual basis.

#20 Influencer

"Brands work with people who contribute to the elevation of their brand in creative and exciting ways."

Igee Okafor, Bond Official

We thought long and hard about including influencers in the matrix of jobs of the digital industry. But even if the economic outlook concerning this function is very uncertain, there are more and more influencers earning their living or generating extra income from it. This function can cover several types of profiles and it seemed to us that it would be interesting to address it here.

We should begin by saying that there have always been influencers. However, they have become more important in the past 10 years with the advent of the digital industry which has accentuated this role and made it measurable. It is no longer necessarily a young, urban girl or woman, who likes fashion and posts on Instagram which is perhaps what most people think about influencers. Today, they are used by brands from all sectors (finance, automobile, etc.), on a variety of digital platforms such as Instagram, Twitch or YouTube, and for very different targets. Influencers also exist in the B2B industry and are now emerging on LinkedIn.

Digital marketing loves metrics and the power of the influencer can be measured according to the amount of followers s/he gathers on the various digital platforms and the rate of commitment of his or her community.

Having gained in maturity, influencers have been placed in the following categories – even though this approach could be considered debatable:

- Nano-influencers typically have less than 5,000 followers. They are ordinary people whose posts can be likened to user reviews.

- Micro-influencers generally have between 5,000 and 100,000 followers and have specialized fields of interest such as fashion or sports. They can earn a living from it, but some simply supplement their income by monetizing their community.

- Macro-influencers have communities of more than 100,000 followers. They are digital natives who knew how to develop a community of online followers very early on or they are well-known personalities such as sports people, actors or TV celebrities. They work with brands over the long term and have significant budgets.

Interestingly, an economy has developed around this phenomenon such as influencer management agencies and tools to identify and manage campaigns.

Estelle Durguerian
Title: Client success director
Company: Obviously
City: Paris
Age: 27

Can you describe your job for us?

Estelle: Obviously is an influence marketing agency. I lead the Client Success team at the agency. We handle all client relations and operational issues. We are the intermediary between our brand clients and the influencers we work with. We are here to design creative influence campaigns, make sure all is delivered on time and that we achieve our initial objectives. I manage a team but as Obviously remains very much a start-up I also define myself as a Swiss Army knife!

What did you do to get into this job?

Estelle: I have a Master in communication. My first professional experience was with Yves Saint Laurent Beauté where I worked in the media team - I was coordinating projects with TV and the press. I went on to work at Tati (a retail brand) as project manager. I worked there on content distribution, social media and in-shop communication.

What do you see happening in this market over the next few years?

Estelle: The advent of social media means we need to be both robust in terms of strategy and technology but also remain agile. We can see a number of new players coming into our market, with different levels of expertise. It will eventually consolidate. Influence is a (very) old business that keeps changing all the time, so it is difficult to tell what the market will be in 3- or 5-years' time.

Igee Okafor
Title: Influencer
Company: Bond Official
City: New York City

What do you do?

Igee: I am the editor in chief of an online men's publication (Bond Official). On top of that I also create social content endorsing products for various clothing and lifestyle brands. Most of my day is spent through emails, calls, in-person meetings and the content creation process itself. I wear many hats. I am a model, producer, art director, event planner, brand ambassador, etc. I work with account directors at agencies, public relations heads, photographers, and videographers. Every time I come up with an idea for a brand, I pitch it to the public relations contact/account director I know. They then usually assist with getting it approved and confirming the scope of work terms. When they come to me with something I didn't pitch, it's up to me to confirm I want to be a part of it. We then agree on a rate to carry out the project with the photographer/videographer depending on what they have in mind.

What are the required skills?

Igee: Definitely communication skills. You need to be able to properly articulate your intention and objectives. Bring a creative point of view because brands work with people who contribute to the elevation of their brand in creative and exciting ways. Being able to prioritize is a skill since you can get burned out with this job - there are a lot of networking, events, deadlines, new projects and emails. You also never know when you will have to end an important meeting early so you can travel for another important opportunity that was presented to you the night before.

What advice would you give in order to be successful?

Igee: There really is no formula. I was running a personal blog with no real intention of making any money. All of a sudden, there were followers and an opportunity to monetize on my own terms but not enough to make a living. I therefore kept a day job only to quit a few years later because the content I was producing allowed it. For someone new at this job, I would advise to look at the first year as an experiment phase. Try to model and figure out what your role is. Taking note of things that don't work around you helps a lot! Adjust as you see fit and ask a lot of questions no matter how inappropriate it might seem. If I had to train someone, I would emphasize on meeting tight deadlines, art directing, and in-person client interactions.

Hannah Power
Title: Personal branding specialist
Company: Powerful leaders
City: London
Age: 27

What work do you do?

Hannah: I work with people to grow their personal brand. I run my own agency, workshops for clients and am launching an academy to train people.

What is your daily routine?

Hannah: I create content for my clients, but also for me as I constantly work on my own personal branding. I also work for clients, manage the team and try to generate new leads through commercial prospection.

What tools do you use?

Hannah: Trello, Canva and Slack plus social media platforms with a focus on LinkedIn.

Conclusion

A Sector That is Growing and Recruiting

The first thing we hear when talking about recruitment in the digital sector is: shortage! Most companies are having a hard time finding people with good experience for the profiles we've covered here.

This means that there are many opportunities out there for those who are interested. These types of jobs are mostly new, so with some basic training and expertise, you can be sure to find a job quickly, with an initial salary that will vary according to the position.

The digital industry offers opportunities in a variety of positions for everyone, with guarantees for those with both analytical and creative profiles.

This of course requires a certain affinity for new technologies, as much as understanding the impact they have and will have on a personal level, as well as on society as a whole. It is important to not lose sight of the final objectives of the job as digitalization is above all a means rather than an end.

Digitalization is having an increasing impact on every segment of activity in our society and the jobs we have described here are applicable to every sector of the economy, from fashion to agriculture, in pharmaceuticals or the automobile industry. You have the opportunity to combine the job of your choice with the sector that attracts you most.

Permanent Changes, Opportunities for All

Some of the jobs we have listed did not exist 5 years ago and may not exist in 5 years' time.

Most of these jobs are constantly evolving which is a guarantee of future opportunities for those who are inquisitive and motivated. Developers will always be open to new programming languages and to new agile ways of working. Sales managers will have to take on board digitalization more and more in order to increase their number of leads.

This means keeping informed about what the day-to-day life of each job involves along with its possible evolutions, which may not ultimately be the direction you wish to go in.

If this is the case, there will still be time for you to change directions towards another one of these jobs but it is better to try and understand beforehand what the possibilities will be in 5 years' time. We believe that there are natural bridges between functions for those who wish to change after a few years. For example, it is not unusual for a content producer to take on the responsibilities of a community manager or for a developer to become a product owner.

It is also worth mentioning that some of these jobs are global, which makes international mobility easier.

A developer can work anywhere on the planet as the languages used are universal such as JavaScript, PHP and many others, as is the case for a UX specialist. This means that being able to speak English is of the utmost importance. However, this is not necessarily the case for a community manager who will need to master the local language or for a sales manager whose job focuses on a network built in the region where s/he works.

What the Main Market Actors Say

Our interviews highlighted a number of trends that should be emphasized:

- **A love of the job**. This came as something of a surprise to us, but the interviewees generally seemed enthusiastic when describing their jobs. More often than not we felt they had a real passion when describing their job which may be linked to criteria other than those they mentioned such as a flexibility due to the possibility of working from home, the sheer adrenaline the job provides (i.e. sales managers), the people with whom they work on a daily basis and whose main goal is the function they work on (i.e. UX designer), being close to technology which is at the very heart of changes in our society or the fact that it is a recent job and much still remains to be invented.

- Most of the people we interviewed believe that **A.I. and automation** will soon have a major impact on their job: sales managers whose leads will be more and more automated, acquisition managers who think they will progressively spend more time on strategy and less on campaign management - which is already mostly done using software. Some do see limits to AI, such as recruiters who believe that humans will remain at the heart of the job despite the tools that continue to improve. Automation may also gain in maturity when maintenance and upfront work are taken into consideration before scheduling reports..

- **There will be more freedom due to the freelancing trend**. Also known as self-employed or contractors in some markets, this trend will increase. Tools for working from home are already widely available. The bigger groups (who are the clients of freelancers) are adapting their mentalities and work regulations accordingly. Some of the jobs we have presented here are already done by independent workers, in particular graphic designers and developers. This is part of the more general evolution of the labor market with the ever-increasing adoption of remote work.

Glossary

A/B testing
Process to test different versions of content or a product feature to measure performance and decide which one to push to a greater audience.

Agile / Scrum
Iterative method of development that helps organizations such as start-ups (but not only) launch new features within short cycles – for example every two weeks instead of every 3 or 6 months.

API (Application Programming Interface)
Connector that allows data to travel between 2 platforms.

BA (Business Angels)
BAs are amongst the first investors in start-ups with amounts from tens to hundreds of thousands of dollars. Their investment usually occurs before a round of seed funding.

CDP (Customer Data Platform)
Tool that helps collect, store and activate all the data a company generates, mostly through interactions with its client base.

Churn
In all businesses churn is the percentage of clients not renewing a contract when it ends (as opposed to the renewal rate).

Design thinking
Design thinking is a process for driving innovation originally inspired by designers' methods. It encourages creativity, focuses on solution-based thinking, brings a social dimension beyond technical perspectives, and promotes collaboration between different teams.

Display
Range of web advertising formats including banners as opposed to text or video formats.

Health score
Scoring system used to evaluate the quality of existing client relations.

KPI (Key Performance Indicator)
Data that helps measure performance (such as an ad campaign).

IoT (Internet of Things)
Describes the network of everyday objects such as fridges or cars, connected and exchanging data over the internet.

Unicorn
A new tech company which is still independent or not yet acquired by a larger group and valued $1 billion or more.

M&A (Merger & Acquisition)
M&A includes all business around the sale of a company. It can be a part of or the entire company. Companies specialized in M&A are often called M&A boutiques or investment banks.

NPS (Net Promoter Score)
Method used to measure customer perception (negative, neutral or positive) of a brand. Developed in the early 2000s by a number of businesses including Bain & Co.

G.D.P.R. (General Data Protection Regulation)
European regulation launched in 2018 that defines the rules of private data usage. The California Privacy Act is the most similar U.S. regulation to the G.D.P.R.

SaaS (Software As A Service)
Broadly used to describe all businesses related to cloud software as opposed to software that need to be installed. The usual business model is a per user (monthly or yearly) licence.

SEA (Search Engine Advertising)
Includes all strategies that help brands to better target and reach their audience through paid campaigns on search engine platforms, mainly (but not only) Google.

SEO (Search Engine Optimization)
Includes all strategies that help brands get better positioned on search engine results, starting with Google.

Soft skills
Soft skills, as opposed to hard skills, are an individual's capabilities not directly related to technical expertise. Soft skills are increasingly considered by recruiters. The ability to code is a hard skill, team spirit is a soft skill.

VC (Venture Capital)
VCs are investment funds that invest in start-ups early in the development of the company with a higher risk compared to other types of funding but with a higher potential return on investment.

Interviewee List

Name	Job title	Company	City
Jose Manuel Martin Sanchez	CRM Manager	Fnac	Madrid, Spain
David Martin	CRM Manager	Cabify	Madrid, Spain
Laura Delange	Project Manager	AccorHotels	Paris, France
Solana Dominguez	Project Manager	Cognizant	Buenos Aires, Argentina
Carolina Nishino	Project Manager	MediaMonks	São Paulo, Brazil
Carlo Mobrack	Project Manager	IBM	Paris, France
Georgia Ingram	Community Manager	Debenhams	London, U.K.
Ariel Cruz Pizzaro	Community Manager	Freelance	Santiago, Chile
Javier del Campo	Community Manager	WWW Digital	Madrid, Spain
Jean-Baptiste Trahin	Growth Marketer	Adobe	San Francisco, U.S.A.
James Arnall	Growth Marketer	Perkbox	London, U.K.
Brice Maurin	Growth Marketer	Deux.io	Paris, France
Omar Odino	Chief Digital Officer	Design group	Milan, Italy
Waël Benkerrour	Chief Digital Officer	Galeries Lafayette	Shanghai, China
Takuji Kawamura	Customer Success Manager	Hubspot	Tokyo, Japan
Stefania Fussi	Customer Success Manager	Yext	Milan, Italy
Nicolas Fatout	Customer Success Manager	Adform	Paris, France
Cécile Eskenazi	Product Owner	Facebook	Menlo Park, U.S.A.
Malick Ndiaye	Product Owner	Knockout Gaming	Málaga, Spain

Name	Job title	Company	City
Marine Suttle	Product Owner	The Boxoffice Company	Los Angeles, U.S.A.
John Knipper	Pre-sales Manager	Gracenote	Berlin, Germany
Brandon DeLap	Pre-sales Manager	Catchpoint	Los Angeles, U.S.A.
Arun Ravuni	Developer	EditPlace	Bangalore, India
Ruslan Bulatov	Developer	Noveo	Saint Petersburg, Russia
Olivier Meyer	Developer	Adobe	Paris, France
Guillaume Martin	Strategic Planner	BETC	Paris, France
Federico Mancin	Strategic Planner	The Big Now	Milan, Italy
Lesly Couty	Strategic Planner	Ogilvy	Frankfurt, Germany
Daniel Kwintner	Strategic Planner	Sopexa	Tokyo, Japan
Cristina Adonizio	Graphic Designer	Freelance	Rome, Italy
Aurélien Foutoyet	Graphic Designer	Freelance	Paris, France
Anouk Szabo	Graphic Designer	ASUS	Amsterdam, Netherlands
Giovanna Gallo	Content Producer	Freelance	Turin, Italy
Omran Omaid	Content Producer	Shopify	Toronto, Canada
Francesca Nicasio	Content Producer	Vend	Los Angeles, U.S.A.
Cristina Padilla	Acquisition Manager	Babbel	Berlin, Germany
Andrea Gonzalez	Acquisition Manager	Go-to Skincare	Sydney, Australia
Mirela Cialai	Acquisition Manager	Zinio	New York City, U.S.A.
Nathan Davies	Recruiter	Marketing Moves	London, U.K.
James Pounder	Recruiter	Michael Page	Tokyo, Japan
Christine Metailler	Recruiter	Talent.io	Paris, France
Élise de Saint-Didier	Recruiter	Executive Search Digital	Los Angeles, U.S.A.

Name	Job title	Company	City
Vinoth Jayakumar	Investor	Draper Esprit	London, U.K.
Virginie Lazès	Investor	N/A	Paris, France
Alex Lazarow	Investor	Cathay Capital	San Francisco, U.S.A.
Juraj Vojnik	UX Manager	BCG	Los Angeles, U.S.A.
Mischa Weiss-Lijn	UX Manager	Google	London, U.K.
Debbie Yang	UX Manager	SAP	Shanghai, China
Thea Backlar	Data Scientist	Ogury	Paris, France
Nicolò Musmeci	Data Scientist	Aviva	London, U.K.
Pawel Goralczyk	Data Scientist	Deliveroo	London, U.K.
Jane Sanderson	SEO Manager	DAC	Toronto, Canada
Elissaveta Tcholakova	SEO Manager	Zalando	Berlin, Germany
Aneel Badyal	SEO Manager	Saatchi & Saatchi	Toronto, Canada
Jessica Lim	Sales Manager	RTB house	Singapore
Ludovic Thevelin	Sales Manager	Google	New York City, U.S.A.
Patrick Amelson	Sales Manager	Xperi	Munich, Germany
Estelle Durguerian	Influencer	Obviously	Paris, France
Igee Okafor	Influencer	Bond Official	New York City, U.S.A.
Hannah Power	Influencer	Powerful leaders	London, U.K.

Interviewee Location

Interviews by country

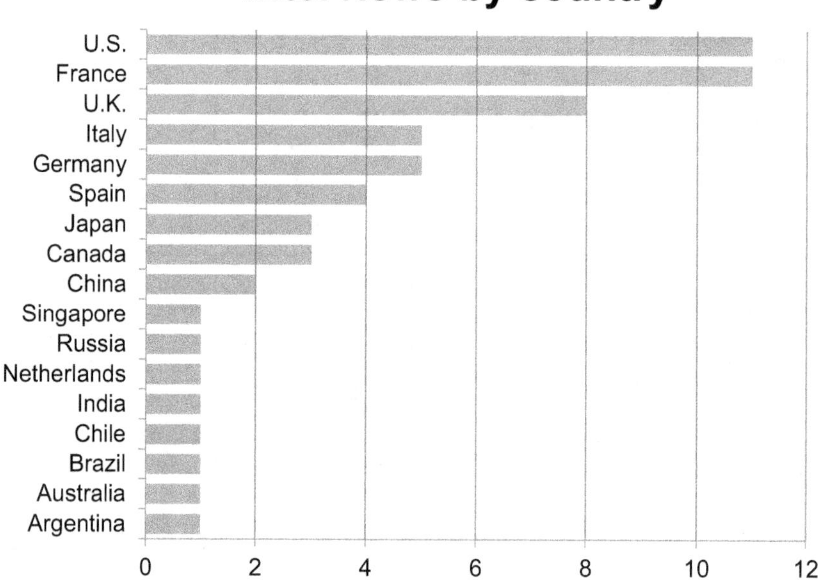

Interviews by region

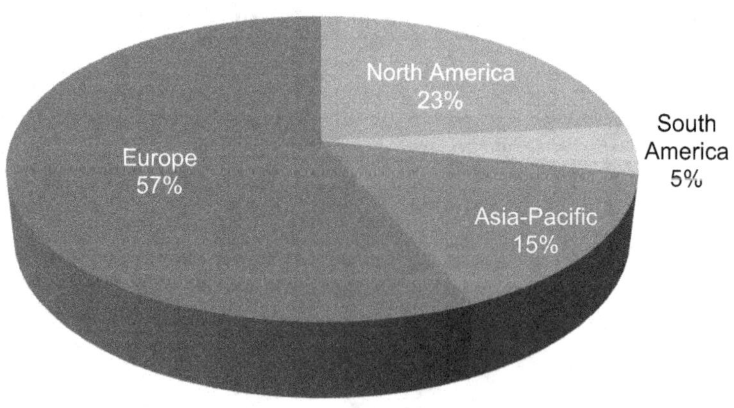

Tools and Services Referenced

This table lists the tools and software used by the interviewees in the course of their work. The tools listed here that do not appear in the final version, having been edited for greater clarity, are shown in italics. The more obvious tools such as email are not listed.

CRM Manager	Braze, Eloqua, Google Analytics, Microstrategy, Neolane, Oracle BI, Salesforce, Tableau, Trello
Project Manager	Adobe Experience manager, Adobe Photoshop, Asana, BaseCamp, Figma, Microsoft Word, Excel, Powerpoint, Sketch, *TeamGantt*, Wise
Community Manager	Asana, Hootsuite, Slack
Product Owner	Adobe campaign, *Confluence*, Google Analytics, InVision, *Figma*, Jira, Mailchimp, Mailjet, *Roadmunk*, Salesforce, Sketch, *Survey Monkey*, Trello, *Usertesting.com*, Wordpress, Zendesk
Developer	Adobe XD and Creative Suite, Angular, BabelJS, Boostrap, CGP, CSS3, Developer Tools plugin for Chrome, Docker, Git, Gitlab, Gulp.js, HTML5, IntelliJ, Laravel, Less, Linux, Node.js, React.js, React Spectrum, Redux, Terminal, Unittest, Vuejs, Webpack, Zend
Strategic Planner	Keynote, Powerpoint
Graphic Designer	Illustrator, InVision, Photoshop, Sketch
Content Producer	Adobe Premiere Pro, Adobe Visual Effects, *Ahrefs*, Asana, *Mangools*, *SEMRush*, Trello, Wordpress
Acquisition Manager	Adjust, Amplitude, Apple Search Ads, Bing Ads, Data Studio, Microsoft Excel, Google Ads, Google Analytics, *Facebook Ads manager*, *Klaviyo*, Outfit, Visual Website Optimiser, *Yotpo*
Recruiter	Crelate, LinkedIn
Investor	Crunchbase, Powerpoint
UX Manager	Axure, Microsoft office, Photoshop
Data Scientist	Fastai, Keras, Python, R, SQL
SEO Manager	Google Ads, Google Analytics, Google My Business, Google Search Console, moz.com, *Squarespace*, *Wordpress*
Influencer	Canva, Trello, Slack

ACKNOWLEDGEMENTS

Our thanks go to all of the people who contributed to this book, especially those who took the time to anwser to our interview requests.

We also thank Sophie Viger, David Honig, and Carolina Milanesi for their contribution which greatly enriched our text and analysis.

Thanks to Céline Bouchez for having designed the cover which, we feel, is a perfect representation of the identity of the book. Thanks to Hélène Fletcher for translating our book.

Finally, thank you to our relatives, friends and colleagues who advised and supported us during these 18 months of designing and writing the book.

www.ingramcontent.com/pod-product-compliance
Lightning Source LLC
LaVergne TN
LVHW050605200726
843508LV00010B/1773